RJ

R. J. Jordan

Running with the Big Dog

True Stories from the Road with
America's Bus Company

Running with the Big Dog

The author may be contacted at:
E-mail: r.jrdn2741@gmail.com

ISBN-13: 978-0615816890
ISBN-10: 0615816894

Dedication

To my girls and the fun we had telling stories at the dinner table.

Too Early for This Much Crazy

It was a quiet morning. We had only been open about 30 minutes. The bus was due out at 7:10 AM. There were only three people in the line waiting to board. And in walked trouble.

She was about 60 years old, 5'-3", with a patch on one eye. On one foot, she wore one of those flat medical shoes. People wear them when they have a bunion removed. As a result, she also used a cane.

The ticket agent, Vanessa, was about the same age and was having a good morning. The lady bought a round trip ticket to Battle Creek. She wanted to leave today on the 7:10 bus. It was now 7:00 AM. The other passengers had boarded the bus. She handed the driver her ticket. At the same time the driver said, "Good morning" and smiled. The lady said, "Take my damn ticket." The surprised driver said, "Okay." He took her ticket, and she went out and got on the bus.

The driver told Vanessa he was ready to leave. She gave him a final boarding call as he walked out to the bus. Once he closed the door, I went back to my office. After about 5 minutes, we noticed the bus hadn't pulled out. As I headed to the bus to see why he hadn't left, the driver opened the door and literally jumped off the bus and ran inside the station. A couple of seconds later the lady with the patch came off the bus right behind him. It looked like she was chasing him. He ran to the ticket counter and said, "She can't ride with me. I'm leaving her here."

He turned around and ran back to the bus. As he did, he passed the lady who was walking as fast as she could toward the counter. When he passed her, she turned around and headed back to the bus. As soon as he got on the bus, he slammed the door before he even sat down. The lady started banging on the bus door. He ignored her and beeped the horn twice, signaling he was about to back up. The lady turned around and put her back against the bus so he could not leave.

By then, I was outside too. I asked the lady to come inside, so we could discuss this. She said, "No, I need to get on this bus. I have a hospital appointment." I walked around to the other side of the bus to talk to the driver through the little window. I asked him what had happened.
 The driver said as soon as he sat in the seat. The lady started harassing him.

"Dang, who cut your hair?"

"You look too dumb to drive."

"Ma'am, I have to ask you to be quiet."

"You ought to ask for refund for that haircut."

"If you continue, I'll have to put you off the bus." "Fuck you, just drive."

That was when he jumped off the bus.

I went back to the lady. Now, she was sitting on the ground with her back against the front wheel. I asked her again to get up and come inside, so we could talk about it. I told her we could put her on the next bus. She said the next bus would make her miss her appointment. I told her she would not be able to ride this bus because of her behavior.

"What behavior?"

"You cannot harass the driver."

"It is a stupid haircut."

"Ma'am, you have to get up off the ground"

"No. He's not leaving without me."

"Ma'am, if you don't get up and come inside, I'll have to call the police and have you removed."

She just looked at me. I said, "Ok" and went back around to tell the driver I was going inside to call the police. The driver said okay.

I went up to the ticket counter and called the police on their regular number, not 911. While we waited on the police (about 5 minutes), the driver got off the bus and came up to the ticket counter and asked, "What did the police say?" I could not believe he'd gotten off the bus!

"What are you doing down here?"

"I wanted to know when the police are coming."

"But if you opened the door, the lady's going to get on the bus!"

"OH SHOOT!"

So we went out to the bus and sure enough, the lady was on the bus. She was sitting there like nothing happened.

Now, I had to try to get her off the bus.
"Ma'am, I have to ask you to step off of the bus."
"Why?"
"You can no longer ride this bus. If you would come inside, we could resolve this and these people could be on their way."
"No. I need to be in Battle Creek for my doctor's appointment."
"Ma'am, I have called the police and if you don't get off the bus. They will remove you."
As I said that, two police cars pulled up next to the bus. I stepped off the bus and explained the situation to the police.

The police boarded the bus and the driver pointed to the lady. They asked her what was going on and she said she needed to go to Battle Creek and we wouldn't let her. She added that the driver had her ticket. So she should be able to go.

I had already mentioned to the officers that we would refund her ticket. They told her she needed to come off the bus with them. She yelled, "No, you can't make me get off!" Then she ripped the patch off of her eye and threw it at the officers. That was the last straw for the cops. One officer stepped behind her to lift her by her shoulders and the other was lifting her by her calves. When they started to lift her, she yelled, "Awww somebody help me. Awwww!" We all just looked at her and did not say a word. Then just as quickly as she started, she stopped yelling and said, "Ok, ok, I'll get off."

She walked off the bus with the officers. I led them up to the ticket counter and waved at the bus driver to leave. I told the ticket agent, Vanessa, to give her a full refund. Vanessa said, "There's a cancellation fee on this ticket." I looked at her like she was crazy. After all this mess, she was going to try to collect the cancelation fee. Really! I quickly, told her to override the fee. I had given the Vanessa the part of the ticket that the driver had pulled. The customer needed to give Vanessa the remaining portion of her ticket. Vanessa asked for the rest of the ticket. The lady said, "No." She then looked at the officer on her left, looked back at Vanessa and said, "He tried to grab my tit." It was too funny. We couldn't help it. We all started laughing. Then I told her in order to get her refund, she had to turn in the ticket. The cops shook their heads in agreement. She paused for a second and looked at us and then gave the ticket to Vanessa. The lady refused to sign the refund stub and I just told Vanessa to give the lady the money.

The officers told the lady she would have to leave the premises. They told her if she didn't leave they would have to take her to jail. She just looked at them. I spoke up and said, "There's a cab here now." She looked at the cab, but didn't move. The cops said, "Okay, let's go ma'am." As the cops reached for her arms to escort her to the door....She dropped to the floor like someone had cut her legs off. Then she started yelling again, "Awwww." When the cops bent over to pick her up, she started kicking and hitting them with her cane. She was whacking them pretty good. They yelled at her to stop. Or they would have to spray her with mace. She just kept yelling, kicking and hitting them with her cane.

Both of the officers pulled out their mace. One cop went to spray her. Just as he started to spray, her cane hit his hand and he sprayed the other cop and himself. All three of them got sprayed! It was like a comedy. Both cops walked outside to get air. They left the lady lying on the floor. The cops took the brunt of the spray. But the lady did stop and sat up. The cops came back in kind of laughing at themselves. They helped the lady up and escorted her to the police car. After they put her in the police car, they took my information and looked in her bags for identification. She had at least 10 different prescription drug bottles in her purse. We guessed that she either forgot to take her medication or took too much.

They opened the car door to ask her about the pills, and she was lying on the seat. They called to her and tried shaking her shoulders, but she didn't move. I thought she was faking, so she wouldn't go to jail. But no one was going to take a chance. The police called for an ambulance. The paramedics put her on a stretcher and took her to the hospital. It turns out she was faking.

After causing an outrageous scene, you would think she would go away and be quiet. A year later, she tried to sue the city. Fortunately, I had a complete record of the crazy incident in my files. The two officers and I had to testify in court. The lady lost her case against the city. The city, in turn, pressed charges against her and she lost.

RJ

The Name Game

Once the bus company began requiring names on every ticket purchased, it was only a matter of time before someone would complain. Initially because of 9/11, no one complained about giving their names. But as time went on, people started to give the ticket agents a hard time. They made comments like," I never had to do this before" or "What do you need my name for?" etc.

Jane was good ticket agent. Under normal circumstances, she handled pressure well and she was good at explaining things to customers. This particular day, she had a customer that did not want to give his name. She explained to the gentleman that names were now required to purchase a ticket. He disagreed and said that she had made the whole thing up. She explained that the change had been made because of the 9/11 attacks. He said, "So what, they didn't blow up a bus!" She said, "Sir, I'm sorry but I can't sell you a ticket if you don't give me a name." He said, "That's a dumb rule, I'm not giving you my ID." She told him she did not need any ID. She just needed a name to put on the ticket. "So I could tell you anything and you wouldn't know if it was right or not." "Yes, sir", she replied. Then he said, "Well, damn, that's just a stupid ass policy, for real. You can put any name you want on it. I don't give a damn. Just give me a got damn ticket." So she did. She typed a name on the ticket, took his money and gave him the ticket and his change. She said, "Thank you and have a nice day sir." He took the ticket and walked over to the boarding door.

When he went to board the bus, he handed the driver his ticket. The driver smiled as he tore it apart. The driver gave back the remaining portion of the ticket. The man wanted to know what the driver was smiling at. The driver smiled and said, "Nothing." As the customer walked out to the bus, he looked at his ticket. Immediately, he yelled out, "Oh, hell no. Where's the manager?" The driver looked at him and motioned over towards the counter. Customer went back inside and told the manager to look at the ticket. The manager looked at the ticket and was extremely surprised. The name the ticket agent had put on the ticket was, first name "Ass", last name "Hole." The manager asked who sold him the ticket. The customer pointed to Jane. The manager gave the customer a free ticket and a refund. He also apologized for the insult. The customer accepted everything and got on the bus.

The manager asked Jane, what she what was she thinking. She said that the man was just so rude. She got fed up and put that on the ticket. She apologized, but the manager fired her. I agree with the manager's decision to fire her. She should have called the supervisor or manager to handle the irate customer. But, I still think it was pretty funny.

RJ

Crazy Love

Some of the driver's wives and girlfriends have been a little strange, but this one took the cake.

This lady walked into the station. She paused and looked around the lobby, as if she was looking for someone. Then she walked up to Burt, at the information desk, and asked if Driver Osborn was there. Burt told her he would check and would return shortly. It is not normal for people to come in asking to see drivers.

Burt returned to the information desk. He said, "I'm sorry, but he's not here." She frowned up her face and said, "I'm his girlfriend and I need to see him." Burt repeated, "He's not here, sorry." She said, "That's bullshit. You guys stick together. I know he's here."

She turned around and yelled, "Got dammit, Eric Osborn, bring your ass out here!!" Security walked up and told her to stop yelling or she would have to leave. She said, "I'm not going anywhere until I see Eric." She strutted through the lobby like she owned the place. As she walked around, she yelled, "Eric, Eric, baby, come on out and get some. You know you like it." Security grabbed her left forearm and said, "Ma'am, you have to leave or we will call the police."

She didn't say a word. She started slowly walking towards the door. After a few steps, she threw her blouse on a chair and started laughing. The customers in the lobby were shocked. Security tried to grab her arm and told her to put her blouse back on. But she slipped his grip and started skipping around the lobby, topless. As she skipped, she kept calling out, "Eric, Ericc, Ericcck."

She continued to remove her clothes and run around the lobby. Of course, the police had been called. Now she was totally naked! She only had on sandals. No one could believe this lady was running around the lobby, completely naked. After a few minutes, she ran out the front door and sat down on the hood of someone's car. The owner, totally unfazed by her nudity, yelled, "Hey, get your naked ass off my car!" At first, she looked at him and didn't move. Maybe it was because she was out of breath. But as soon as the owner started to walk towards her, she jumped up laughing. She turned to walk away and a female cop grabbed her arms. The cop put her in the car, got her clothes and drove away. What a show!

RJ

The Entrepreneur

Jesse and Sara had been around buses for 40 years. Jesse was a bus driver and Sara worked in the accounting office. They met in the bus station cafeteria and had been together ever since.

No one knows how they came up with the idea. But at some point, they decided to open a charter bus business. They had run their business for at least 10 years before it collapsed on itself. One phone call killed their business.

A customer called the main office to see if anyone had turned in the cooler they had left on the bus. The customer had ridden on a chartered bus to Six Flags. Her call was transferred to the Charter Department. The Charter Department did not have a record of a Six Flags charter out of Columbus. They asked the customer if she had the right company. She had the bus number, the driver's name and described the logo on the side. The Charter Department apologized but they could not help the customer.

The call did trigger an investigation within the company. Turns out Jesse and Sara were using the company buses for their own business. Sara would set up a charter for Jesse's day off. Jesse would put on his uniform and go to the bus company's garage and pick up a bus. Since he was in uniform everyone thought he was working. So no questions were asked. He would then use the bus for the charter his wife had set up. If he needed fuel during the charter, he would simply stop that any fueling point and they would fill the tank and charge the bus company and no one was the wiser. Their charter business made 100% profit!!! It was unbelievably simple and crazy. They realized no one was really keeping track of the buses or the fuel. As long as he looked official, Jesse could run charters any time he wanted.

When their scam was discovered Jesse and Sara were fired. No one knows how much money they made. But they got to keep it! They were only fired the bus company never sought restitution. They probably have an estate on a tropical island, now ☺

RJ

Payback is a "B"

Sometimes, bus drivers can be mean, just for the sake of being mean. In those cases, it's nice when they get paid back. The payback may not be pretty, in fact, it may be cruel. But sometimes it's justified.

Driver Rodriguez was always short with the customers. We all figured he was just not a very nice person. He would do his job but he was not nice. Smoking has not been allowed on buses for years. So when Driver Rodriguez caught someone smoking in the restroom, he had every right to put the passenger off the bus.

When the bus pulled into the Lincoln Park station, Driver Rodriguez told the young man that was smoking he had to get off the bus. Now, Lincoln Park is only 30 minutes from the main station downtown. The young man was surprised and asked the driver if he could have another chance. The young man said, "We're almost home, I won't do it again." The driver said, "No. I told everyone when we started our trip there was no smoking on the bus. And if you were caught smoking on the bus, I would put you off. You were smoking in the restroom. So you have to get off." The young man was angry. He told the driver it was dumb not to let him ride on to downtown. The driver said, "Oh well" and got back on the bus. The guy asked, "What about my bag?" The driver said, "Too bad. You can pick it up downtown." The guy yelled back at the driver, "Come on, man. Give me my damn bag." The driver closed the door and drove off. Company policy is very clear when a person is put off the bus, the driver is supposed to give them their luggage.

The young man immediately pulled out his cell phone, as the bus drove away. The driver was rather pleased with himself. (No one knows how they pulled this off) Right after the bus pulled into the dock at the main bus station downtown, a green car pulled up behind the bus. It stopped short, screeching it's brakes! As the driver stepped off the bus, four young men jumped out of the car! The baggage men had begun taking luggage off the bus. The young man who was left in Lincoln Park, walked up to the driver and said, "Hey, remember me?" As the driver turned to face him, the young man punched the driver in the face. Then, each of his three friends punched the driver in his face and he fell to the ground. It happened so fast that it was over before the baggage men realized what had happened. A couple of customers screamed. The young man that was left in Lincoln Park grabbed his suitcase and said, "You should've given me my got damn bag! And they sped off in the car.

The security guard ran out onto the dock and the police were called but it was too late. Nothing could be done to stop the guys. They were gone, and no one knew who they were. When the ambulance came, they determined that the driver's jaw was broken. The driver was out for six weeks. When he returned, he had a slightly better attitude and was a little more pleasant with the customers.

I don't condone violence. But, I do think the driver got what he deserved. If he had given the young man his bag, the incident would have been over. The young man knew he was wrong for smoking, but the driver was wrong for not giving him his bag.

RJ

W T F ?

Linda had been working at the station for couple of years. She was a pretty happy person with a pleasant attitude, perfect for dealing with the public. The restrooms in the station were very clean and well maintained. (One of the perks for small station).

On her break, Linda went into the ladies restroom. While Linda was in one stall, she heard someone else come into the restroom and go into the adjacent stall. After a minute or so, a bloody used tampon came flying under the dividing wall of the stalls!! It just missed Linda's foot and splooshed against the wall. Linda yelled, "Hey, what the hell!" The lady in the other stall said, "Oh, I didn't know anyone was there." Before she could catch herself, Linda yelled, "What's wrong with you? That's fucking, nasty. Why couldn't you just put it in the container in your stall, that's what it's for!" The lady didn't answer.

As Linda walked out of the stall unable to avoid looking at the mess she wanted to wait for the lady to come out so she could say more to her, but she decided against it and went back to work.

Dealing with the public can be a mess!

RJ

The Bonehead Award

It was 6:00 AM and I was short staffed at the terminal. I didn't have a morning baggage guy and my morning ticket agent called in sick. But that was ok; I could run things alone for a while. I had already prepared yesterday's cash for the Brinks pick up. I figured, I'd sell a few tickets for this first bus and when the bus left I would run the reports. No problem, this would be a good day.

My first customers were an average couple and seem happy. The guy was carrying the suitcase. Right before she turned to face me at the window, he gave her a kiss and sat the suitcase down in front of the counter. He said, "Call me when you get there." She smiled and said "Ok."

As soon as she faced me, I said, "Hi, how can I help you?" She said, "I need a ticket to Cleveland, OH."
"One way or roundtrip?"
"Roundtrip."
"Are you planning to leave this morning?"
"Yes, at 7:00 AM"
"Do you have any luggage to check under the bus?"
"Yes, one" (She pointed to the suitcase the guy sat in front of the counter).

"Alright, one roundtrip ticket to Cleveland, leaving at 7:00 AM, today and returning in one week. Is that correct?"

"Yes"

"That'll be sixty two dollars."

She handed me the exact amount in cash. I entered it in the system and the ticket printed.

Now, I was in a good mood and things were going well, despite being short staffed. And the bus was pulling up right on time. The first piece that prints out of the ticket printer is the baggage claim check. (Policy dictates that customers take their luggage to the side of the bus when they board). I separated the two pieces of the claim check. As I stapled her portion of the claim check to the ticket envelope, I told her:

"This is your claim check to pick up your bag when you get to Cleveland."

"Ok."

"Since you're pregnant, I'll take your bag out and put it on the bus."

"I'M NOT PREGNANT!!!

I could've died! She gave me the dirtiest look. She was pissed. I said, "I'm sorry" but there was nothing I could say to fix it.

I put her bag on the bus but it didn't matter. She would hate me forever. Damn!!! I don't know what made me say that. I've never said anything like that before or since. What a bonehead.

RJ

Stairway To Heaven

It was a typical fall day. The sun was shining which was rare at that time of the year. This location was the oldest property in my group. Frank was a very good manager. He treated the customers well and knew the business. The building did not do him justice. The old terminal had been built back in the 40's. It had seen better days. The roof leaked and the electricity shorted out from time to time. In the winter, it was cold and drafty.

The restrooms were on the second floor at the top of the stairway. We reduced the men's room down to one stall and one urinal. At one time, there were four stalls and three urinals. The plywood that blocked the unused portion was painted blue but the old restroom just looked bad. The ladies room wasn't much better. It had a seating area without seats and two stalls reduced from four. It just looked old and worn out.

Frank and I were standing at the bottom of the stairs discussing bus service. A couple walked by on their way to the restrooms. The girl was in her early twenties with a light blue velvet like sweat suit. The guy, also in his twenties, had on baggy jeans with a black leather jacket and brown t-shirt. There was nothing special about the couple. After they passed, we continued our conversation.

All of a sudden, Frank said, "Did you hear one or two doors close?" I said, "I wasn't paying attention." Frank said, "Just one. Come on, watch this." We went up the stairs and walked into the women's room. In the first stall, you could see two sets of feet. Frank knocked on the stall door and said, "Hey you guys can't do that here, you've got to leave." We walked out of the restroom and waited at the bottom of the stairway. A couple of minutes later, they came out of the restroom. The girl walked passed first. She had pulled her blue hood over her face as if she was embarrassed. But the guy strutted pass like he wanted to brag. It's amazing they wanted to have sex in those old, disgusting restrooms. Wow!

RJ

Bonnie and Clyde

You have to watch everyone when you deal with the public. People are more tolerant of senior citizens. That's the human characteristic Bonnie and Clyde counted on.

It was winter time, about 10 PM. 10 PM was our busy time. We had four buses arriving from various parts of the state. Most passengers on those buses transferred to three other buses waiting at the terminal. This took place back when we used to transfer the luggage from one bus to another. Now, customers transfer their own luggage. There were customers everywhere. One of the baggage guys stopped me and said, "There's Bonnie and Clyde." I said, "Who?" Of course, I heard what he said but I didn't know what he meant. I had only been working there a few months and hadn't seen them before.

He pointed to an elderly couple boarding the bus. The man had crutches and the lady was helping him up the steps. They looked to be about 80 years old. The baggage guy said, "They're pickpockets. They ride between Toledo and Cincinnati on stolen tickets. They only ride when it's crowded. When they bump into people (because of the crutches), they pick their pockets. They make a fortune."

But, since they hadn't done anything, I had to leave them alone.

After the bus finished boarding, I went on the bus and made the following announcement, "May I have your attention. We have received a tip that there may be pickpockets on this bus. We do not know who they are. But just in case, keep a close eye on your belongings. Have a nice trip and thank you."

A few weeks later, at the same time of night, I spotted them crossing the lobby heading for the Toledo line of passengers. This time, I cut them off and asked if I could help them. They said no and tried to step around me. I asked them where they were going. They said,

> "That's our Cleveland bus. We need to get on."

> "Since the bus has started to board, you'll have to wait until the other customers have finished boarding. We board customers with disabilities first. But if you arrive after boarding has begun, you have to wait until boarding done. We do this for your safety. If you'll have a seat, I'll come and get you when it's clear."

I would not let them go to the front of the line. It was obvious they were pissed at me!! If looks could kill, I'd be dead. The man looked at me and said, "Fuck you, man" and walked away. As he walked away, he put both crutches in one hand. In the seating area, he threw his coat and crutches across to chairs and went into the restroom.

That became our routine every time I saw them in the building. Eventually, when they would see me, they would just leave the building. And every time they saw me, they cussed me out under their breath. We all got a kick out of foiling their plan.

RJ

The Girl is Mine

A Driver Manager once told me, "The girl goes with the room." He was making reference to the "girls" that work the rooms where the driver stay on the road. As you might imagine, our drivers stay in hotels all over the country. Usually, the hotel will designate a room just for our drivers. In this case, they got more than clean sheets.

Driver Martin and Driver Johnson were good buddies. They had gone through driver training school together and been friends for a long time. They had both bid on the run to Marion. They worked in rotation. When one driver was off, the other driver took his place. They decided that since they used the same room at the hotel, they could leave some personal items there all the time. They split all of the storage space in the room 50-50.

Driver Johnson had a girlfriend in Marion. Whenever he spent the night there, he'd call his girl Loretta. They had been seeing each other for about a year. One night they were watching TV in the room and Loretta spilled something on her blouse. Not thinking, she got up and went over to the dresser. She opened one of Driver Martin's drawers and pulled out another blouse. OOPS!! Driver Johnson was surprised and asked her, how did she know a blouse was in there? Loretta paused then said, "I left it there, last time, just in case. Don't you remember?" The problem was Driver

Johnson did remember. He told her, "The last time I was here you wore a t-shirt and jeans. You didn't bring anything extra!" She said he was right. She didn't want to upset him. She told him, "Sometimes, I stop by when Driver Martin is here. There's nothing going on between us. We'll just have dinner from time to time."

Driver Johnson did not believe her. He yelled, "If you only have dinner from time to time, why do you have extra clothes in his dresser?" She tried to act insulted by asking, "You don't believe me?" But he wasn't buying it. He accused her of sleeping with both of them. And trying to fool him into believing they had a real relationship. At this point, Loretta knew she was caught and started laughing. She said, "A relationship? Are you in high school? We see each other a couple of hours a week and don't talk in between visits. You've got to be kidding!!! A girl's got needs." He didn't know what to say. Driver Johnson was angry and hurt. But he knew she was right. He was the dumb one, thinking there was more to it. Trying to save face, he told her to get out and he would take it up with Martin. She kissed him on the cheek and said, "Don't be mad baby" and left.

Driver Johnson was livid. Driver Martin was his buddy. How could he sleep with his girl behind his back and smile in his face every day? When Johnson questioned Martin, Martin admitted it. Martin was surprised Johnson didn't know. Driver Martin told Johnson, "We all hit that when we stay in Marion. I'm not the only one. Come on, now be serious. You're married, how serious could you be with her?" Now Johnson was embarrassed and angry. Martin laughed right in his face and told the other drivers. They all had a good laugh at Johnson's expense. And they, including Driver Johnson, continued to see her when they were in town.

Driver Johnson was still angry. So, he reported to the Driver Manager that Martin allowed a woman to stay with him when he was in Marion. That is against company policy. Driver Johnson was playing the innocent role. He complained, "I shouldn't have to stay in a dirty room." He didn't think we knew what was really going on. The Driver Manager asked me to investigate. So I did. As soon as Driver Martin heard I was checking the Marion hotel, he called me. It was funny. He played innocent, too. He did not want this rumor to get back to his wife. He denied the story. He said Martin was pissed about a car sale gone wrong and was looking for payback.

The only thing my investigation found (that could be proven) was that they both were leaving personal items in the room. And the hotel had been cleaning the room daily but allowing the drivers to leave personal items. They were both told to remove all of their personal items when they checked out. I removed all of the personal items that were in the room when I was there. I gave them to the Driver Manager. I also asked the hotel to treat any personal items left in the room like they would any other room. On my way out, the porter said to the clerk "Is Loretta part of the room?" and started laughing.

Driver Johnson tried two more times to use the room situation to get back at Driver Martin but it didn't work. Loretta had to stop seeing Driver Johnson because he couldn't handle it. No one knows what other drivers she may or may not have been seeing. On the next bid, Driver Johnson bid a different run. Johnson and Martin are no longer buddies. Now they don't even speak to each other.

RJ

The Family Business

Life on the road can be pretty interesting. This happened somewhere in the middle of the country. I was riding with another Area Manager and it was lunchtime. We decided that we would stop at a strip club for lunch. This was not normal but it had been a slow day and we decided it would be interesting. We had no idea how interesting.

There were only a few people in the place. It was a small place. It was clean and well lit. If it wasn't for the sign in the window that said, "Strippers", we would've thought it was a regular little diner. We walked in and the lady said, "Have a seat gentlemen, I will be with you in just a moment." She was sweeping behind the bar. She came over to our table with two menus. She asked if we would like something to drink. We both said coffee and a glass of water. When she came back, she said the show would be starting shortly. We both ordered a sandwich, nothing special. The lady said, "My daughter is a pretty good performer." Surprised, we both said, "What?" She said, "My daughter performs here. This is a family business. I taught her everything she knows. Her father's the cook." She smiled and walked away.

We could not believe it! We never imagined that a mother and daughter would be working at a strip joint. And the father is the cook. Wow! The lights were lowered on the small stage. The music started and out came a nice-looking young lady, in a bikini. She danced around the pole and chair. Her moves were about what you'd expect. After a few minutes of dancing, she removed her top and continued to dance. About the same time, our waitress came back with our sandwiches. She was beaming. She said, "What did I tell you, she's pretty good. Don't you think?" We both had an uncomfortable look on our face and nodded yes. She asked us if we needed anything else. We shook our heads no. She then told us that she had to go change because it is almost time for her to perform. All we could do was shake our head. We could not believe what was happening!

Sure enough, a few minutes later, the daughter came down and introduced herself as our waitress. A new song started to play, and out came the mom dancing on the stage. She was actually a better dancer than the daughter. The whole situation was funny to us. It made our day. Who would've thought the family business would be a strip club, on the side of the road, in the middle of nowhere. We left nice tip. Here we thought it would be a little different to have lunch at a strip club. It was more different than we ever imagined. But, it made us laugh.

RJ

What Customer Service?

It was a typical summer night in Columbus. Customers were riding the buses and happy to get to their destinations.   Anthony was an elderly gentleman probably in his mid-70s. He had gray hair and a grandfatherly manner about him. This was a regular bus trip for him. He took this trip at least twice a month.   So he was really familiar with the inner workings of the station. But tonight was different. He did not recognize this driver and the driver seemed to have a bad attitude.

The passengers had boarded the bus and were ready to go.   The driver got on the bus and began his announcement.   As part of his announcement, the driver said that he did not want to hear anyone talking during the trip. All of the passengers looked up and said, "What?" The driver repeated that this was a long trip and he did not want to hear anyone talking. He said it was his bus and he could decide who was going to ride and who would not. The passengers looked at each other in disbelief.   But, I think, most of the passengers figured he just wanted a quiet ride.

There were two young ladies riding together that looked to be in their late teens or early 20s. They began to giggle because they did not believe that the

driver could tell them not to talk. Then the driver
spoke directly to the girls that were giggling. He said,
"You girls need to be quiet or I will put you off the
bus." The girls said, "You can't tell us not to talk. We
aren't your children." The driver said, "That's it, get off
my bus!" The girls looked stunned and did not move.
He said he was going to go get security to remove
them from the bus. Then he left.

No one could believe what just happened. You could
hear little discussions all over the bus about how
outrageous the driver had been to the girls. Anthony
turned around and asked the girls if they would mind if
he handled it when the driver returned. The girls were
surprised but said sure. Anthony said, "This driver
can't put you off the bus and I will tell him that."

The driver returned with security. He told security, the
two girls needed to be escorted off of his bus. Security
said, " Ok, ladies, let's go." Anthony stood up and said,
"Wait a minute. The driver cannot put these ladies off
the bus for talking." The driver said, "This has nothing
to do with you, old man, sit down or you'll have to get
off the bus, too." Anthony responded, "No, I won't. I
haven't done anything, and neither have they."

 Then Anthony made his demand. He told the security
guard and the driver that "As paying customers, we
demand a new driver! We do not want YOU on our

bus." All of the customers on the bus cheered and clapped their hands. You could hear different voices saying, "Yea, that's right. We want you off the bus." Security and the driver were both surprised.

Anthony demanded a supervisor be brought on board and the driver be replaced. He told them that the customers on this bus refused to allow this driver to take them anywhere. And they were not getting off the bus. They wanted a new driver. Security left and brought back a supervisor. The supervisor was stunned and did not, really, know what to do. This was a new situation for the supervisor. The driver, security and the supervisor left the bus. After a few minutes, the supervisor came back on the bus and told everyone they would get a new driver. The passengers all cheered and clapped for Anthony. The supervisor had a smug look on his face and said, "But it's going to take two hours to replace the driver. The choice is yours. You can go with this driver or wait for a new one." They all said they would wait. The stunned supervisor said ok and left.

The girls told Anthony thank you. They appreciated him standing up for them. Several other customers on the bus condemned the driver's bad behavior, as well. After about 20 minutes, the supervisor brought pizza out to the bus for all the customers. He apologized for the driver's bad behavior and said that a new driver should be there in 30 minutes. The new driver arrived approximately 30 minutes later and took the passengers to their final destinations.

This is a good example of what can be accomplished when people stand against unfair treatment.

RJ

Too Funny

This particular day had been pretty uneventful. No real issues. No crazy problems. A customer came in and asked the ticket agent for refund. The policy is very clear. To get a refund, you need ID and your name has to be on the ticket. Of course, you need the ticket.

The ticket agent asked the lady for her ticket. The lady said, "This is all I have." She handed the ticket agent, the ticket receipt. The ticket agent said, "This is not the ticket. This is just a receipt. I need the actual ticket." The lady said, "Here's my ID, I bought the ticket." The ticket agent said, "Ma'am, I cannot refund the ticket without the ticket." The lady said, "This is bullshit. I paid for the ticket, and I want my money back." Ticket agent apologized but again refused to give the refund.

The lady asked for the manager. The ticket agent came and got me. She explained what the problem was and said that the lady was pretty upset. I went up to the counter and asked the lady what seemed to be the problem. The lady said, "That bitch won't give me my refund, that's the problem." I said, "There is no need to use foul language. Let me see what you have." The lady handed me a ticket receipt and her ID. I asked her where was her ticket. She told me that was what they had given her when she purchased it. I told her that was the receipt and that the ticket was attached to it. She said, "That's all they gave me and I need my got damn money!"

I told her we could not refund her money without the ticket. She went ballistic! She said, "This is bullshit. You motherfuckers better give me my money. I hate this place. There's always some bullshit going on when I come here. They need to close your stupid ass down." Then she started to bang on the counter while she yelled, "Give me my got damn money." Once again, I told her I was sorry but we could not refund her money without the ticket. She continued, "Who the fuck are you to keep my money? You think you're some kind of big shot. Well, you ain't shit."

At this point, I had enough. I told her she would have to leave the property, because we could not help her. She said, "I'm not going any damn, where. Fuck you!" I told her if she didn't leave, I would have to call the police and have her removed. She looked me in the eye and said, "Well, ain't that about a bitch!" I didn't say anything. I just stood there looking at her. It was weird. None of us were upset. She had cussed so much, it was like a performance. Good for us, there were no other customers in the building at the time.

She finally turned and walked away from the counter. When she opened the door to leave the building, she stopped, turned and looked at me and yelled, "You

Urkel looking motherfucker!" That was it, we all started cracking up. It was just too funny.

Now for those of you who don't know who Urkel is. Urkel is a character from the old ABC TV show, <u>Family Matters</u>. Urkel wears big glasses and is the ultimate nerd. Well, I'm short and I wear glasses so that made it very funny. That was one of the best laughs we ever had. It caught all of us off guard. It was a great line ☺

RJ

Hats Off!

Ted had been driving a bus for 10 years. He had an excellent driving record and he considered himself a player. He was 5'- 8'' with black hair cut short. His hair curled around his ears. He liked being tan but he had a hard time keeping his tan. He weighed about 250 pounds with a potbelly. He rarely had good luck picking up women for the night but in his mind, women couldn't resist him.

Tonight, Ted had to take the bus from Columbus, OH to Pittsburgh, PA. He would have to spend the night in Pittsburgh and drive the return trip to Columbus tomorrow afternoon. No big deal, he had done it several times.

He thought to himself, (Damn, I'll be glad when I get to Pittsburgh. It'll be nice to see that cute girl at the front desk. I'm getting it, tonight. I've thought about it long enough. Tonight, she's mine. I'll be there for 10 hours and I only need one to get the job done.)

"Ok folks, this is our rest stop. We'll be here for 15 minutes. Your bus number is 1520. That's 1-5-2-0. There will be another bus here before we leave. So remember, 1-5-2-0 so you don't get on the wrong bus. Please watch your step." (Hmm…25 people).
(Alright, 25 people back on). "Ok folks, we are about to leave for Pittsburgh, PA. If Pittsburgh is not your destination, please come forward now. You are on the wrong bus. Remember, this is a non-smoking coach. Please do not smoke in the rest room. We're almost to

Pittsburgh and I'd hate to put anyone off the bus. Now just sit back and enjoy the ride."

The trip was uneventful. Ted made it without any problems. All 25 people got their luggage and were on their way. Ted just had to get something to eat and go to bed at the hotel.

(There she is. Damn, she's fine 5'-5" about 120 pounds and a great smile. Oh yeah, she's mine tonight.)

"Hi. I need the driver's room key for tonight."
                "Yes sir, I just need your
        company hotel card and you'll be all
        set."
"Well, what do you have planned for tonight?"
                "I'm going home and have
        dinner with my husband. Here's your
        key. Your room number is written here.
        We serve breakfast right behind you
        starting at 6:00 AM until 10:00 AM. Is
        there anything else I can help you with?"
        "Yeah, is there a resturant near here where I
can get something to eat?
                "Yes sir. Just one block down is a nice
        family diner. Turn left out of out of our drive,
        you can't miss it."
"Have you eaten there before?"
                "Yes."
"How's the food?"
                "It's very good."

"I could use some company. Why don't you call your husband and tell him you have to work late."

" I don't think so. You have a nice night, SIR!"

" You said the food was good. Don't you want to try some dessert?"

" No, you go ahead. Have a nice night, sir."

Frustrated, Ted went to his room and changed clothes. The red hat he put on was his favorite. He was convinced she was afraid that she wouldn't be satisfied at home, anymore, if she had dinner with him. So he was better off that she turned him down. He didn't need a clingy girl pissing off his wife. He drove the bus off the lot and turned left toward the resturant.

He drove right pass the resturant and went straight downtown. He stopped the bus two blocks away from the USA Bank. Ted liked this bank because they had a night deposit box for small businesses. Ted had worked for USA Bank before he began driving the bus. While he was there he found out how the lock system worked on the night deposit boxes. He stayed on top of the system changes through the years.

As he walked towards the night deposit box, he pulled his favorite red hat down low so you could not see his eyes. Whatever, Ted wasn't worried. He knew what he was doing. When the bank discovered the theft, he would be long gone. He would be on his way to another city with a bus load of happy passengers.

As he walked up to the night deposit box, he kept his head down. He put his homemade gadget on the lock. He heard the "click" and knew he was in. He put the all of the contents in his sports duffle bag, closed it door and walked away. Five minutes, five thousand dollars. Not bad for five minutes work. Ted was beaming.

At the hotel, it was time for shift change. Sarah briefed Jessica on the days' events as usual. She made a point of mentioning the the driver.

"Girl, watch that bus driver. He was trying hard to get me to be his dessert."

What??? No way, the regular guy."

" Yep. Gross!"

"I know, right."

" You'll see him soon enough. He went to Clair's Diner. Have fun. See you tomorrow."

"Ok, night."

On the way back to the hotel, he stopped at the resturant and picked up dinner. When he got to the hotel, he thought, DING, DING round two. He lifted his red hat and smiled, so his 5'-8" 140 pound victim could see how good he looked.

"Good evening. Damn, you're fine! How 'bout you come to my room on your break?"

" No sir we're not that kind of hotel. Besides I would get fired."

" I won't tell if you won't tell."

" Have a good night."

"You're probably married, anyway. Hey, what happens in Pittsburgh….."

" Have a good night, SIR!"
" Your loss!" Ted went to his room disappointed.

It had been a quiet night. So the lobby TV helped the time pass quicker. Breaking news….. the downtown USA Bank branch had been robbed. Police said the silent alarm had been tripped. They said if anyone had seen this man, please call the police.

When she saw the photo, Jessica was schocked. (Oh shit, that looks like the bus driver. That's the same kind of red hat he had on. No way, that would be crazy. Where's my phone? Come on, Sarah answer the damn phone. Don't nobody want you to come to work). "Hello..Sarah..hmm. Wake up!!
         "Who is this?"
         " Jessica at the hotel."
      "What, damn! I'm sleep."
         " Look at the news!!! I think the bus driver robbed the bank. They have his picture on TV!"
      "So, what chu want me to do? Whatever, bye!"

Jessica called 911 and told them what she thought. It wasn't long before the Police arrived. They went to the driver's room but didn't find anything except the red hat. Then they checked bus. After an hour, they found $5000 hidden behind a panel in the luggage bins. The driver was arrested.

After further investigation, the police discovered he had robbed 10 other banks in 10 cities!

RJ

Artistic Freedom

The corporate headquarters for the big bus company was in Arizona. The daughter of the head of the big bus company attended a Midwestern college. Of course, the big bus company had a station in that college town. A lot of people aren't aware of it but the big bus company also ships packages. The packages are shipped under the bus with the luggage.

The CEO decided that he wanted to send his daughter a painting for her dorm room. The painting was approximately two feet by three feet. By using the package shipping department of the big bus company, he could send it for half-price. No big deal. Employees shipped packages every day using their employee discount.

The CEO gave the painting to the Head of Shipping and asked him to ship it to his daughter. The package was delivered to the downtown station for shipping. The local shipping salesperson was told to ride the bus with the package to the first transfer point. The first transfer point was Little Rock. In Little Rock, the Area Manager was to meet the bus. He was to take the painting to the transferring bus and ride that bus to the next transfer point. The next transfer point was St. Louis. In St. Louis, the Terminal Manager was to take the package to the new bus and ride with the package to Chicago. In Chicago, the Shipping Sales Manager was to ride with the painting to the final destination in Ohio.

Can you imagine being pulled off of your regular job to ride the bus with a package? Then to have to wait in the transferring city for a bus to return you home. Most of the guys involved with the package spent two or three hours in the transferring city waiting for their bus to go home. They were frustrated because it was silly. The drivers could handle the package with no problem. They do it every day.

Needless to say, the package made it without a problem. The CEO sent an e-mail to the Head of Shipping, patting him on the back because the package arrived with no problem. In the e-mail, the CEO commented that he could not understand why more people did not ship packages. "The service was great." The head of the shipping department forwarded the e-mail to all of the managers involved an added his own words of thanks. Of course, it was nice for the Head of Shipping to relay the thanks to everyone involved. But it was also funny to most of us because of all the man-hours used to ensure a flawless delivery. It was like the Secret Service was planning for presidential visit.

Don't get me wrong, the big bus company does do a good job shipping packages. But the CEO seemed a little naïve, if he thought his daughter's painting was handled like every other package. It's good to be boss.

The Stranded Family

The bus station is located right by the freeway exit. One day, in front of the terminal, I noticed a guy with a gas can approaching our customers as they were taking their luggage out of their cars. He was just a regular guy. He did not look like a bum or anything like that. He was clean-shaven, with regular casual clothes.

I went outside to get his story. As I approached him, I could hear what he was saying to the customers. He was asking the customers for gas money. He told them he had run out of gas on the freeway. His wife and daughter were waiting in the car and he'd appreciate it if they could spare a few dollars so he could get some gas. Of course, the lady he was asking felt sorry for him and gave him some money. I told him I understood his situation, but I could not allow him to ask customers for money in front of our door. He was nice and said he understood. He looked at the money in his hand and walked away.

The very next day, he was back! I couldn't believe it! He was a hustler. There was no wife and kids on the freeway. By looking normal and not bummy, he could ask for money without raising suspicion or fear. It was the perfect scam.

Every time he would see me or security heading his way, he would leave. This went on all summer. I can only imagine how much money he actually made hustling our customers. I bet he made $10,000 that summer. Think about it. When people give gas money, they rarely just give a dollar.

RJ

Pistol Packin' Mama

Anderson is just a small town. And the bus station was small too. It was a small one-person operation. The lady that ran the station was just a sweetheart. She was always friendly. She always had something positive to say. Her son was on the local police force. As a result, her son had recommended a pistol for her to keep at work, just in case something happened. He also taught her how to use it. No one would suspect that she knew how to use a 9 mm pistol.

Jennifer ran a nice little station. She did Western Union, UPS, FedEx, sold money orders and did Bill Pay, in addition to selling bus tickets. So she had steady traffic. It was rarely crowded but steady.

This particular day was uneventful, just like all the rest. About one in the afternoon, a guy walked in and jumped over the counter. Jennifer was surprised and jumped back away from the counter. As he jumped the counter, he pulled out a pistol and said, "Give me the money." As she jumped back, she grabbed her pistol and pointed it at him! He was totally surprised! He did not expect that. He said, "Oh shit" and fired a shot at her. She shot back. He jumped the counter and ran out. She shot at him one more time as he was running out and missed. She thought she had been shot. The bullet he shot whizzed right by her left ear, and lodged in the wall. It went by so close that she felt it pass. Of course, she called the police and four police cars showed up. They never found the guy and everyone was glad she was not hurt or robbed. Her husband was a good carpenter. After this incident, he built a Plexiglas screen to prevent people from jumping the counter in the future.

About two months later, about 3:00 PM, a guy came into the lobby. As he walked into the lobby, he began shooting. We think he was trying to shatter the Plexiglas so he could jump the counter. After the first shooting incident, Jennifer kept the pistol right at the counter out of the view of the customers. So when the guy walked in the door shooting, she grabbed her pistol and immediately shot back. The guy turned and ran. He had shot at least four times before she shot back. She was not sure if she hit him or not. She had shot at him five times. The police told her she may have grazed him because there was a little bit of blood on the sidewalk.

The shootings were the talk of the town. No one could believe in two months, there were two shootings at the small one-person bus station. Even more surprising was Jennifer's response to the armed gunmen.

She got the nickname "Pistol Packing Mama". It is amazing that no one was shot. The area of the shooting was only about 10 square feet. I called it, "The Gunfight at the Anderson Corral." No one has tried to rob the station since that last shooting. I think the word has spread that she has a pistol and is not afraid to use it.

RJ

Was It Worth It

Tessa was a very good employee. She was very friendly and pleasant. She smiled a lot and was always on time. After working with her for a few months, I began to think that she might be a good long-term employee.

One day, Tessa came to work and said that her car had broken down. She had a mechanic look at it and it would cost $700 to repair. She complained that she did not have an extra $700 to get her car repaired. She had just purchased school clothes for her two daughters. She talked about her broken down car all week to anyone that would listen. So by the next week, all the employees knew her car had broken down, and it would cost $700 to repair.

Sometimes, you wonder what people are thinking. For her to be so nice and so professional, I was really surprised that she could be so dumb. Plus, she had told everyone how much it would cost to get her car repaired.

We had two computers. One for sending Western Union transactions and the other one was for selling bus tickets. The bus ticketing computer kept a record of everything that was done that day except the Western Union transactions. Whenever a ticket agent would send a Western Union, they had to enter the transaction into the bus ticketing computer, too.

One morning as I was reviewing the reports for the previous day's business, I noticed a discrepancy in the reports. It was exactly $700. There was no Western Union form for a $700 transaction in anyone's report envelope. Tessa had worked the night before and her report was the one that was out of balance. Part of the reviewing process included comparing the report from the Western Union computer to the report from the bus ticketing computer. Apparently, Tessa did not realize that. There was a $700 Western Union transaction that had been sent with Tessa's password. But the $700 was not in her cash. I double checked everything to make sure that I had not made a mistake. It looked like Tessa had stolen $700. But I didn't want to believe it. She had been such a good employee. But I had been surprised before, and it was very obvious what happened.

When Tessa came to work, she was all smiles. I heard her in the back telling one of the employees that she had gotten her car fixed. I could not believe what I was hearing! I called her in the office and asked her about the missing money.   She said, she did not know anything about a $700 Western Union. I asked her if at any time during her shift, if she left the counter and forgot to sign out of the computer. I was hoping maybe someone else had used her computer to conduct the transaction. But, her answer was no. She did not leave the computer unattended and signed on. I asked her if she noticed any other employee at the counter. She said no. I told her it looks like she mishandled the $700. The Western Union transaction was done under her password. The Western Union transaction had not been entered into the bus ticketing computer. And, the transaction was done during her shift. She was the only ticket agent last night. I asked her if there was any other possible explanation for the missing money. She said, "I am not going to lie on anyone. I don't know what happened to the money." I told her, "Ok, go back to work."

It was obvious that she had stolen the money. I went to the police station and explained the situation to the officer on duty. He told me to go talk to the detective. I explain everything to the detective, and he agreed. It looked like Tessa had stolen the money, even though I didn't want to believe it. The next day, the detectives came to the bus station to interview Tessa. I asked Tessa to step into my office. I told her these two gentlemen were detectives from the police department, and they wanted to talk to her about the missing money. They started asking her questions about the money. They pointed out that only her password had been used, and she was the only one behind the ticket counter when the transactions were done. She just looked at them with a cold stare and didn't say a word. They repeated the information they had, and asked her to explain. All she said was that she didn't know what happened.

The detective was tired of her giving him the runaround. He stood up and slammed on the desk and said, "If you didn't take the money, then what happened to it?" It was just like something out of a TV show. Her expression changed. It was like night and day. She said, "Fuck you man. I didn't take, shit. And you can kiss my ass!" I was totally surprised and convinced (at that moment) that she had taken the money. Her expression made it clear that she had dealt with the police under these circumstances before. We had done a background check when we hired her. And it came back clean. But they only checked in Michigan. It turns out that she had been arrested several times before in Mississippi and Alabama.

The police told her to stand up. They put the handcuffs on her and took her to jail. The other employees were all surprised and shocked. It was so crazy. Now, her daughters would have to go into foster care because she was under arrest. I could not believe she would risk her family for $700, but she did. Because the amount was over $500, she could get sentenced to up to 10 years in jail!! It just was not worth it. How stupid.

A few weeks later, I had to go to court for her case. I was sitting in the witness waiting room for about 30 minutes. The District Attorney came in and told me that I would not have to testify. Tessa had admitted guilt and would be sentenced accordingly. She received six months in jail and she had to pay restitution to the bus company. During the six months, her daughters were put in foster care. Tessa had been a very good employee, but stealing is stealing. She knew what she was doing, and chose to do it. She had no one to blame but herself. What a disappointment.

RJ

Pin the Tail

Barbara had been driving for least 20 years. She was known as a driver with a short fuse. She had cussed out customers and agents along the road before. She had been suspended several times during her career. She had problems with several agents along her run because of her attitude.

She did not get along with the agent at the bus station in Crown Point. Over the years they had several arguments. Jeffrey, the agent in Crown Point, felt that she should have been fired a long time ago. When she would pull into his station, they would not speak each other. They both did their jobs and went their separate ways. This arrangement seemed to work well for both of them.

This particular day, Barbara was running late. So needless to say, she was rushing trying to make up the time. When she arrived in Crown Point, the customers came out of the building and met the bus. As soon as she opened the door she yelled at them to go back inside. She told them she would not take tickets outside. The six customers turned around and went back inside. They were irritated that she yelled at them. Jeffrey asked them what was wrong. They told him that the driver told them to come back inside. Jeffrey went outside to see what was going on. As soon as he stepped outside, Barbara yelled that she did not want to hear any crap from him. He told her that he had just come out to see what was going on. She said it didn't matter what was going on. It was not his business.

As he turned to walk back inside, he said, "You're crazy." She heard him and came in right after him, yelling, "Don't you call me crazy!" He just looked at her and kept walking. She grabbed him by his shoulder and spun him around. Then she said, "Did you hear me? Don't you call me crazy." He yelled back, "Don't touch me." The customers looked at both of them like they had lost their minds. They were acting like two kids. They both repeated themselves, "Don't call me crazy." "Don't you touch me, again!"

Jeffrey said, "Get your tickets and get your crazy butt out of here." Barbara said, "I told you" and she grabbed Jeffery by the arm. He pulled his arm away from her and pushed her back with his other hand. Barbara stepped back and reached up to her hat. She pulled out a hat pin about six inches long. She didn't say a word. She stepped forward and stabbed Jeffery in the stomach with the pin. The customers all gasped in surprise. Barbara left Jeffery on the floor and said, "Who's going with me on the bus?"

One customer called 911 on her cell phone. Another customer said to Barbara, "You stabbed him." Barbara looked at him and said, "That's why I keep this pin in my hat," as she gestured to her hat. Barbara said,

"Who's going with me?" All the customers just stood there shocked that she did not seem to be phased at all.

Two police cars pulled up and you could hear another siren off in the distance. The police came into the building and ask what was going on. Several customers pointed at the driver and said, "She stabbed that guy." One officer went over to Jeffrey lying on the floor and the other officer went over to Barbara. The officer asked Jeffrey, what happened and he said, pointing to Barbara, that she had stabbed him. Barbara told the police officer handcuffing her that she did stab him, after he attacked her. The ambulance arrived and took Jeffrey to the hospital. The police took Barbara to jail. The police also contacted the bus company and told them what happened at the station. The bus company had to send another bus out for the customers.

A few days later, Jeffrey and Barbara filed charges against each other. The bus company reviewed the security tape and terminated Barbara. After Jeffrey heard that Barbara had been terminated, he dropped his charges against Barbara. But he did not realize, Barbara did not drop the charges she had filed against him. Jeffrey was found guilty of assaulting Barbara and given two days in jail and six month probation!!! He could not believe he was stabbed, but had to go to jail!

Since Jeffrey dropped the charges against Barbara, the Driver's Union filed a grievance on Barbara's behalf. It took a few months, but Barbara got her job back with back pay. Wow, is that crazy or what? OOPS, I better not say crazy ☺

RJ

TRULY TERRIBLE

This story is very sad. It is the story of how several coincidences came together to create a tragedy. This happened on a clear summer day in small town USA.

The station in Bowling Brook was just a small place. It was located in a small strip mall. No parking was allowed on the front side of the mall because it was on the main street. The parking lot was behind the mall. Almost all of the traffic for the mall came from the parking lot, which was never very busy. The bus also used the parking lot. The bus would pull up right in front of the bus station to load and unload. In the mall was a beauty shop, a party store, a book store and a small hardware store.

The bus pulled into the lot in Bowling Brook, the same way it had done hundreds of times. There were only about four cars in the parking lot. It was around 11:00 AM. The bus was an old MC-12 model. The front and rear bumpers on the MC-12 buses stuck out about 6 inches from the actual bus, creating a small ledge.

The driver was loading and unloading the bus as usual for the four people that got on the bus and three that got off. The driver had gone inside the bus station to touch base with the agent to make sure he had everyone. The two of them had a nice quick conversation and he was ready to go. Before he got on the bus, the driver walked around the bus to make sure everything was clear. The driver got on the bus and closed the door. Just as the bus began to move forward, a customer ran up banging on the side of the bus. Normally, once a bus begins to leave the station, the driver will not stop for late customers. This particular day, the driver was having a great day and decided to stop for the customer. The driver opened the door and the guy said, "I know I'm late, thanks for stopping. I just need to run inside and get a tag for my bag. I'll be right back." The driver said okay and smiled.

At this exact same time, a female senior citizen had pulled into the parking lot to go to the hairdresser. While the man was inside getting a tag for his bag, the lady who had to be about 4'-7", was walking towards the beauty shop. After my investigation, this is what I think happened.

The beauty shop entrance was closer to the rear of the bus than the front of the bus. I have no idea why the lady decided to walk around the front of the bus instead of the back. As she approached the bus, she decided to steady herself by leaning on the front bumper. As a result, she was right up against the front of the bus. The customer came out of the bus station with a tag for his bag. He put the tag on his bag. The driver stepped off the bus, and put the bag in the baggage compartment. The driver took the customer's ticket and they both got on the bus. The driver closed the door. The lot was clear in front of him. He put the bus in gear and drove forward. As soon as he pulled forward, he heard a scream. He was startled and stopped the bus immediately! The customers on the bus all looked out of the windows to see what was wrong. But they didn't see anything. The agent at the bus station came outside because she heard the scream, as well. As the agent came out of the bus station, she was horrified. She screamed, too. At the same time, the driver was stepping off of the bus to see what was wrong. The agent yelled, "I'm going to call 911"and went back inside to make the call. The driver could not believe what he was seeing. The senior citizen that was going to the beauty shop had been run over by the bus, literally. There was blood everywhere, and the lady was taking her last gasp for air. It was absolutely terrible. There was nothing anyone could do to help the lady. The driver held her hand and cried.

The fire station was located directly across the street from the bus station. The ambulance and fire department were there within 2 minutes, but it was too late. The lady had passed away. The Police came, too. Of course, everyone was removed from the bus and taken into the bus station. And the bus company was called. The police and firemen roped off the parking lot to prevent onlookers from getting too close.

Needless to say, everyone was extremely upset. The driver was not charged for the accident. There was no way for the driver to have seen the lady because she was right up against the front of bus. The driver never returned to driving. I can only imagine how terrible he feels about that day. And there is no way to understand how terrible her family feels. She was simply going to get her hair done.

The newer model buses do not have a ledge type bumper. If they had a newer bus, this tragedy may not have happened. If the driver was not trying to be nice and kept going after he closed the door the first time, this may not have happened. If the late customer had come on time, this may not have happened. If the lady had decided to walk around the rear of the bus instead of the front, this tragedy may not have happened. If the driver had decided to walk around the bus before he left, as he did the first time, this may not have happened. As they say, hindsight is twenty-twenty. But, what did happen was a series of coincidences resulting in tragedy.

Hey Buddy

Bill was a great agent. He ran a very nice one man bus station, he had become an agent after retiring from driving the bus. The whole town knew and liked him.

One day a guy walked into the station. Bill said, "Hi buddy, how can I help you?" The guy said, "I'm not your damn buddy!" Bill was a little surprised. But, he just smiled and said, "In my book, you can be a buddy or an ass hole it's up to you. So which is it?"

The guy was stunned. He then said, "Hey buddy, let me get a ticket"

That was the best response ever.

RJ

Time to Go

Driver Underwood is a big guy. He is about 6'-5" and he weighs about 400 pounds. The schedule he was driving would take about four hours from start to finish. His schedule left at 1:00 PM. He was the regular driver for this schedule, which means he drives it every day. He had been on this schedule for about two months.

Now, there is a restroom in the hotel and there is a restroom in the bus station at the starting point of this schedule. In fact, there is a restroom in all eight stations along the route. There is also a state rest area between two stations. Remember, the total travel time for this trip was four hours.

Driver Underwood pulled the bus out on time. He made the standard announcement, no smoking in the restroom, no loud music and be kind to your neighbor. It was a sunny day and everyone was happy.

About one hour into the trip, the bus stopped at a station located in a strip mall. It was a small strip mall. The bus simply would stop in the parking lot between the rows of parked cars. The driver would pick up and drop off passengers and keep going.

This time the bus stopped right in from of the Department of Motor Vehicles. The DMV office had floor to ceiling windows facing the parking lot. The driver exited the bus and walked to the station. There were no new passengers waiting to board the bus. The driver walked around the outside to the back of the bus.

He opened the doors to the engine compartment. The doors opened to the right and left, meeting in the center. After he opened the doors to the engine compartment, he proceeded to take a piss. Yes, right there in the middle of a strip mall parking lot. He couldn't have done more to draw attention to himself. The big bus sitting there and the driver at the rear of the bus, taking a PISS!! Right in front of the DMV!

The people in the DMV office were shocked. They called the police and reported what they had seen. By the time the police arrived, the bus was gone. The police chased the bus down and stopped it on the freeway. They issued the driver a ticket for an improper stop in the parking lot. They also sent a formal report to the bus company. But, since they could not prove he had taken piss in public, they could not do any more.

RJ

Almost Legal

I was tired and ready to go home. It had been a long day. My evening ticket agent did not show up so I had to stay and sell tickets. It was 9:30 PM. We closed at 10 PM and I was counting the minutes. The last bus had arrived and all the passengers had left the terminal. We were just wrapping up things before closing.

This girl came through the door that looked like she had been crying. Her mascara was running and her clothes were dirty. Her jeans were too long and were worn out around the bottom. She came up to the counter and said she needed to get on the next bus going out. I told her there were not any more buses, today. The next bus wouldn't leave until 7 AM. Her face just dropped. She said she needed some help, that someone was after her. When you work with the public a lot, after a while, you can usually tell when people are lying. And it didn't seem to me that she was lying. So I brought in the baggage room and told her to have a seat. I sat her in a chair away from any windows so she could not be spotted from outside.

I asked her what was going on and who was looking for her. She said she had been working the street for a while and was tired and wanted to go home. She was trying to get away from her pimp. She said she had run away from him and now he was looking for her.

She said she did not have any money, but she wanted to go home and needed help. Then she started to tear up. It wasn't a full-blown cry. It was more like sadness had overwhelmed her.

I told her to sit there for a moment while I wrapped up a couple of things. I went back out to the counter to check the lobby and make sure things were fine. Right as I was doing that, a girl walked in the in the front door. She had just gotten out of a car that had the headlights off and just had the turn signals on. I thought that was strange, and figured it must be the pimp. The girl walked through the whole terminal looking in every corner. Then she went into the ladies restroom came out and never said a word. By the time she had come out of the restroom, the car was at the back of the building. She walked out the rear door and got back in the car and the car drove off. I wrapped up the few things that I needed to take care of and told the baggage man to lock the doors. I explained to him what was going on. Before I had finished talking to the baggage man, the same car drove around the building a second time.

I told the girl what I had just seen. She described the car and we agreed it was probably her pimp looking for her. I told her I would call the police and see if they could help us. I called the nonemergency number for the police department. I identified myself to the officer and told her that I had this runaway girl at the bus station looking for help. I added that I thought her pimp had come to the station looking for her. And I thought the girl was telling the truth. The officer paused and then asked me a series of questions about the girl. The officer described exactly what the girl looked like. I was surprised! Then, the officer asked me, "Is her name, Sharon." I asked the girl if her name was Sharon and she replied, "Yes." The officer said, "I'm sorry sir, but we cannot help you. In fact, we will not help her." I asked the officer, "Why not?"

The officer told me that she had come to them earlier in the week with the same story. They asked her a few questions and went and picked up the guy, her pimp. After they picked him up, Sharon began to tell them lies. They caught her in several lies and had to release the guy. The officer said, "Once people lie to us, they are on their own." She said there was nothing else they could do. I asked her if she could give me the phone numbers for a few of the women shelters in the area. The officer gave me the numbers and then hung up. I told the girl what the officer said and asked if it was true. She said, "Yes." She had gone to the police. And yes, she had lied to them. She said, "After that, he beat me and refused to feed me. The last couple of days have been horrible. He fell asleep and I ran away. Now, I really do want to go home."

All I could think about was what if this was my daughter that had run away from home. I would hope someone would step up to help her. So that's what I wanted to do. She did seem remorseful, but that might've just been fear. After talking to the police, my guard was way up but I was still going to try to help her. I sent the baggage guy home. No need for both of our night's to be ruined.

I called the first shelter on the list. I told her who I was and asked them if they could help me with this girl. The lady on the phone had the exact same reaction as the police. She described the girl completely and said, "No, we cannot help her!" The lady actually seemed kind of angry. The lady went on to say that the girl had been there twice before and each time lied and then came back. They were no longer going to help her take assistance from women that really wanted help. The lady said, "Sorry sir, but we are done with her." I asked the girl, "What the heck were you thinking, lying to the people that can help you." She said, "I didn't mean to." I told her, "You don't lie by accident."

I called the next number, and the exact same thing happened. So, I called the third number and SURPRISE the same result. Now, I didn't know what to do. This girl had pissed off all the organizations that could help her. So what was I supposed to do with her now that she changed her mind and really wanted help?

The bus company sells "Prepaid Ticket Orders" or "PTO." A PTO is a bus ticket paid for in one city and picked up in another city. The person picking up the ticket can have ID or they could use a password to pick up the ticket. I asked Sharon if she had any family that could buy her a ticket and she could pick it up here. She said, "No, it's just my mom and sisters and they don't have any money. They don't even have a phone." Again, I thought, what would my daughter do in the same situation? So, I asked the girl if she had any friends back home whose parents know her and might help her in an emergency? I thought if my daughter's girlfriend called me in an emergency situation, I would try to help her and contact her parents. She said she did have a buddy that lived down the street that might help. I asked her for their information.

It was about 10:30 PM, so I hoped they wouldn't be too angry with me for calling so late. A man answered the phone. I identified myself and told him that I had Sharon sitting here in my office. He stopped me in midsentence. My heart dropped. Not again, I thought. Yep. He was very nice and took the time to explain to me what was going on. He said about a year ago, Sharon had run away from home because she no longer wanted to follow her family's rules. He said she had a mother and father and two sisters. They live down the street and it was a typical middle-class family. She just did not want to follow the rules. He said, over the last six months, he had received at least six phone calls just like mine. The first couple of times, he did buy the ticket and told her parents. They went to the bus station and she never arrived. They confirmed that the tickets were picked up, but she never made it. Her parents were at their wits end. They didn't know what to do to get her home. I asked him if he could give me their phone number and he said, "No." Although he did believe me, he had given their number out before and they were taken advantage of by Sharon and her acquaintances. He said he was sorry that he could not help but please do not call again.

Now, I was angry with Sharon. I told Sharon, "I don't know what kind of game you're playing, but I'm tired of it. You have lied and cheated everyone that has tried to help you, including me! You said at your house there were only your mom and your two sisters and they were too poor to have a phone! Apparently, all of that is a lie. I think, I should just put you outside and let you fend for yourself." At that, she broke down and cried. She really cried. She admitted that everything I said was true. She didn't know what to do now because she had nowhere to go and was frightened that the pimp would kill her, if he caught her this time. She said she was sorry and would not lie anymore. She asked me to please help her.

I told her, ok. But now she had to answer my questions, truthfully. Anymore lies and I would put her out. I asked her what her parent's names were. Then I asked for their phone number and she gave it to me. I called her parents and explained what was going on. They were very grateful that I called. They had no idea where she was. She had called them from all parts of the country. She actually lived in Pennsylvania. They wanted to help her, but they had been in this spot before. They explained that they would no longer send her any kind of money. I could not believe what I was hearing this girl had burnt every bridge she had. Her parents made it clear that she was welcome to come home and they would be glad to have her back. But because of all the scams she has pulled on them, they would not help her get home. I thanked them for their time and told them that I would let them know what happens and hung up.

So I asked her, "What am I supposed to do, now?" I told her, "You can't stay here and you're NOT going home with me! She was balling now. I yelled at her, "STOP CRYING. YOU CREATED THIS MESS AND CRYING DOESN'T HELP. SO STOP IT!!" After a couple a minutes, she stopped and I got an idea.

I called the first shelter and asked the lady if she would let the girl stay overnight. The lady's first reaction was a flat, "NO." I explained to the lady that I felt that Sharon had learned her lesson. I told her that I would be willing to give Sharon a bus ticket home. But the bus did not leave until the morning and I did not have a place for her to stay. I asked the lady if she would please allow Sharon to spend one night there. After a long pause, the lady said, "Ok, but if she gives us any problems at all. We are going to put her out in the street. Do you understand?" I said, "Yes ma'am, thank you." I told Sharon, what the lady said, and she started to smile.

While I had the lady on the phone, I told Sharon, this is probably her last chance to get it together. The lady at the shelter asked me, "How is she going to get here and back to the bus station. We are not paying for anything. She's lucky we're letting her stay here." The bus company had an account with the local taxi service. I told the shelter I would give her a voucher to get to the shelter that night and one to return to the bus station in the morning. I would come to the bus station, first thing in the morning, an issue Sharon a ticket if she was there. I told Sharon, "If you are not here for that bus in the morning, don't come back looking for any kind of help." She said, "Don't worry. I'll be here."

The bus was due out at 7 AM. I was at the bus station at 6:15 AM. 6:30, no Sharon. 6:45, no Sharon. 6:50, still no Sharon. I could not believe it. She was going to screw this up, too. I told myself that I had given her my best shot. I was a little disappointed, too. I really thought she was going to show up. 6:55, no Sharon. At 6:56, she pulled up!! I could not believe it! It was so funny because I was really excited that she made it. I got on the P.A. system and told the bus driver to wait. She jumped out of the cab and ran to the counter. She still looked crappy. At least, she had washed her face. Wow!! She might have been 17, and that's a big might. I walked her to the bus and gave the driver her ticket. She gave me a big hug and started to cry. I told her, "Don't cry. You're making the right decision. Just learn from this experience and move forward. Take care of yourself." She thanked me again and got on the bus. The driver had a strange look on his face. He had no idea what was going on.

I went inside and called her parents. I gave them her arrival time and told them where she should transfer buses. I told them how we handled everything. They were very thankful and said they would keep their fingers crossed that she would come home. A few days later, I called them to check and see if she had made it. I was kind of surprised that they hadn't called me. But not really, surprised. They were happy. She had made it home, safely. Sharon got on the phone and thanked me for the money for food. She sounded like a completely different person. It was amazing.

RJ

Creative Solution

As an Area Manager, part of our job requires us to stay in hotels from time to time. The company decided to save money and take advantage of some of the new technology by having us do more work from our offices. They instructed us to try to spend less time on the road. "We want you to reduce your windshield time." They wanted us to use the new technologies to accomplish the same job and reduce the expense of hotels whenever possible. The Area Manager Group thought this was a wonderful idea. Since, we spent most of the time on the road. We were more than happy to try to make it work.

But there was a problem. Some in upper management felt that if we were not on the road, we were not working. That course of thought would've been true, if it was 1970. Of course, we were caught in the middle. After a few months, our boss questioned why we were not spending more money on hotels. On a conference call, we all said the same thing. "We thought you wanted us to reduce our road time to save money and improve our quality of life at home. Did we misunderstand, you?" Our boss said, "No, that's exactly what we said." But as time went on, any time, our hotel bills were lower than they used to be, we were questioned. Most of us had grown tired of the mixed messages and the harassment over the hotel bills.

After being pushed to the limit, about half of the national Area Management Team, decided to go back to the old way and run high hotel bills. Everyone's hotel stays increased nationwide. The harassment stopped almost immediately. But what the company did not realize was they forced the group to figure out another way to accomplish the same goal. When possible, managers would check into hotel on a Tuesday and then go home. They would return a few days later and check out. By doing this, they stopped the harassment of upper management for low hotel bills and improved their quality of life at home. The funny thing is our work did not suffer. Our productivity actually improved. The solution seemed to be an unnecessary waste, but that's what happens when a company punishes the employees for saving money. They must have forgotten part of our job was to solve problems. Problem solved.

RJ

Stalled

This happen before the Americans with Disabilities Act became law.

The bus had arrived on-time without incident. As I approached the bus, I noticed the driver bringing a customer into the building in a wheelchair. The man in the chair looked about 25 years old. He had on jeans, a black T-shirt and a black leather jacket. He had a rather sad look on his face, too. As the other customers deboarded, the driver rolled the customer over to me. The driver told me the guy needed help going to the restroom.

I grabbed the wheelchair handles and said, "Hello Sir, I can take you over to the restroom." He did not respond at all. I propped the restroom door open with my right foot and rolled the customer in his wheelchair into the restroom. There was one stall and one urinal in the restroom. The stall was ADA accessible, which meant it was a lot larger than a regular stall.

I rolled him into the stall and turned his chair around to a position I thought would make it easier for him. I was guessing because he did not say a word. I told him I would wait outside and I'd be back to check on him shortly. Again, he didn't say anything, nor did he do anything to let me know that he understood. As I stepped away, I reached back to close the stall door and I noticed him trying to unbuckle his pants. This was the first time he had moved. He could not straighten his wrist. And, he clearly did not have any strength in his arms or hand. It made me sad because I could only imagine how I would feel in the same condition. So I said, "I can unbuckle your belt for you, if you want." He just looked at me. I unbuckled his belt and unfastened his pants. I stepped away and said, "I'll wait outside this door." I pointed to the stall door. Once again, as I closed the door, I noticed that he did not move at all. At that point, I realized he could not use the restroom without help through the whole process.

I was pissed! How could his family put him on the bus, alone? Most strangers would not do this. And I wouldn't expect my employees to help someone to this degree, either. Not only did I need to help him with his pants; I needed to move him from his wheelchair to the toilet. Fortunately for me, he was a thin guy. I repositioned his chair so I could lift him to the toilet. In order to move him to the toilet, I had to straddle him. His legs were in between mine. If it wasn't me, it would've been funny. I could just imagine what it would look like to someone walking in the restroom. Here are two guys in the stall facing each other. And the one sitting down, has his pants open! What a crazy image that would have been!!

When I tried to move him over, something was stopping me. I checked to see if his jacket was caught on the chair. It wasn't. I could not move him all the way over. What was wrong? Why couldn't I move him? I thought, I must need to use more strength. Maybe, I was being too careful, because I didn't want to hurt him. So this time I pulled him up with a lot of force. I tried several times to move him. Jerking him up, pulling and pushing him, nothing worked. He still had not said a word. I stood up, totally baffled. Then I look down and noticed his legs were all crisscrossed over each other. HOLY CRAP!!! His legs were caught in the foot rests on his chair the whole time! He didn't say anything. I guess because he couldn't feel it. I don't know. What the heck was he thinking? He could see! But he never said a word. This was ridiculous. I felt like an idiot. I uncrossed his legs and moved him with ease. I stepped out of the stall while he did his business.

When he was done, I fixed his pants and got him back in the chair. I had to lift him up twice because, the first time, his jacket caught on the back of his chair and ended up around his head. Goodness gracious! I fixed his jacket. Now, he was ready to go back out. We stopped at the sink and washed our hands and headed for the door. I was so glad no one came in and witnessed that fiasco. But it turned out okay. And, the guy was able to use the restroom.

I propped the door open with my foot and rolled him out into the lobby. As soon as he was in the lobby, he yelled, "MA!!" at the top of his lungs. It startled me because he had not spoken the whole time! This lady that was looking out of the window, turned around and said, "Here I am." She walked over to us. When she stepped behind his wheelchair she almost knocked me out of the way. She said, "Ok" and they left! They never said thanks. They didn't smile. They didn't even say move. They just left.

I couldn't believe it. She had ridden on the bus with him. She was there the whole time. You know, she could have helped him use the restroom better than I could. She probably helped him all the time. Maybe that was it? She wanted a break and she got it.

RJ

How Is This Possible

My area had been expanded to include the State of Illinois. I had been going around visiting the new locations, introducing myself to my agents. On my first visit, I usually was not very critical. I would use the first visit as an opportunity to get to know the agent's thoughts and feelings about the bus business. This visit blew my mind.

The station was located in a small town near St. Louis. It was an old motel. It was only two stories tall, but it covered about 4 acres. I could tell at one time it was a very nice motel right off the freeway. But the days of it being a nice place to stay, passed years ago. The place did appear to be clean, even if it was pretty old.

I noticed there were several notes taped to the front door. I didn't stop to read them. I was surprised that there was a person sitting on the floor, right behind the front door. The motel entry way was about three feet square. You open the first door, turn to your right and go through the door into the lobby. Both doors were made of glass with an aluminum frame. Standard doors you'd see on most businesses. As I walked across the lobby, I noticed one man sitting at a table. The lobby seemed to be set up for customers to eat breakfast. There were several small tables and chairs around the lobby. And a TV attached to the wall in the corner. I did notice the coffeepot had a sign above it that said, "Hotel patrons free coffee. Bus customers one dollar." The sign surprised me because this was the bus station. How could the agent only charge bus customers for coffee?

I stood at the front desk waiting for service. I knocked on the counter and said hello, trying to get someone's attention but no one came to the counter. After about two minutes another customer came into the hotel and stood behind me. We looked at each other and smiled and continued to wait for someone to come to the counter. After a couple more minutes, the man that was sitting at the table in the lobby got up and walked behind the counter! I couldn't believe it! He worked there! He had been sitting there watching me from the time I walked in and never said hello. Nor did he come to the counter when I was looking for service. He had no idea who I was or where I was from. As I said, I could not believe this. To make matters worse, when he came up to the counter, he asked the gentleman behind me if he could help him, not me. I didn't say anything because I was there as a bus employee, but if I had been a customer, he would've had a problem.

After he finished with the other guy, he asked how he could help me. I introduced myself to him and asked to see the owner. His demeanor changed immediately. He stuck out his hand to shake my hand and said, "I'm the owner. I'm the bus agent." He said he'd seen my name on the correspondence I had sent notifying them that I was now in charge of his location. He offered me a seat at the table where he had been sitting, when I walked in. I asked him how was business. He said his business was not bad but he was sick of the bus customers. He went on to tell me that someone had broken into the motel the night before. I asked him if anything was stolen and he said no. Just a broken window and the damaged bus sign.

I asked him what he meant by his statement that he was sick of the bus customers. I said, "Running a motel you deal with the public a lot. How are the bus customers any different from the general public you deal with for your motel?" He started on a rant. He said things like, "The bus customers stink. They are dumb. They steal." And then he said he did not allow them to sit in his lobby. I interrupted him and said, "What, what do you mean they cannot sit in the lobby?" He then said very clearly, "Once they buy their ticket, they have to leave the building." Then he got up and walked towards the door. He said, "Like this guy." He pointed to the guy sitting on the floor just inside the front door. He said, "This guy is a bus customer." I said to him, "I don't understand. Why is he sitting on the floor?" (Just so you know, it was raining outside that day.) The agent told me he was sitting on the floor because he had told the customer he could not wait in the building. And his bus was due out in 30 minutes. I COULDN'T BELIEVE IT!!! The customer looked like a monkey in the cage. I just remember that was my first impression. It was like the customer was at the zoo on display. INSANE!

I told the agent, "You can't treat customers like that." He asked me what did I mean. I told him he was the bus station in this town. He's making a commission off of selling bus tickets. Why would he think he could discriminate against his bus customers and be the bus station? He told me that I should be glad that he was doing it at all. He said, "Those bus people are just a pain in the butt." He continued, "There is a picnic table outside under the tree. He can sit over there if he likes." I told him that was unacceptable. AND it was raining outside. He simply did not seem to care at all. I motioned to the guy to come inside and sit in a chair and he did.

So I asked, "What if a customer had to go to the restroom?" He said, he tells them there isn't one. He said his note on the door, clearly tells the bus customers that there is no restroom and that they cannot wait in the lobby. I went to the door and read the sign. Not only did the sign say there were no restrooms. It clearly stated that bus customers could not use the lobby, could not stand in front of the building and could not wait to pick up passengers near the building. The sign even asked if they would park on the far side of the parking lot and wait for the bus. It was the worst bus station I had ever seen.

I went inside and told him he would have to change these things. I told him it was unacceptable to treat customers this way. And, if he wanted to continue as our commission agent, he would have to take down all of the signs restricting bus customer's movements. He said when other people from the bus company had come to visit they didn't say a word about his signs. I told him, "It did not matter, all the signs had to go or he could not be our agent." I could tell he didn't like it, but he said okay, and started to take the signs down.

I left quite upset. I could not believe this man had been allowed to be our agent! Nor could I believe that other people from the bus company had visited and thought everything was okay. But what took the cake for me was our District Manager lived in that same town! How is that possible, the District Manager could live in the city with the worst bus station in the district? I thought about the bus station all weekend. Monday when I went to the office, I decided the station had to go. I felt that if that was the best we could do in that city, then we should not have a bus station there.

Our standard commission agent's contract has a 30 day termination clause. Either party can cancel the contract with 30 day's notice. The only way to get around the 30 day notice would be in the case of theft.

This station was so bad I didn't care. I was going to take my chances and cancel the guy's contract.

I drove out there first thing Tuesday morning. The first thing I noticed was that all the signs had been put back up. I guess he did not think I was going to return. When I walked up to the counter, he had an odd look on his face. After seeing the signs had been reposted, I knew I was making the right decision. I told him I had come to accommodate him. That he made it clear he did not want bus customers on his property. So as of right now, I was canceling his contract and would need to collect the company's property from him. He was shocked. He said, "You can't do that. I have a contract. You have to give me 30 day's notice to shut me down." I said, "I don't care, if you want to sue, then sue. But as of right now your contract is terminated, and I'm taking the property that belongs to the bus company." He said he was not going to give me anything. I told him I didn't want to call the police. But, if he would not give me the property, I would. He demanded a phone number for someone above me. I gave him the District Manager's, office phone number. I knew no one would answer that line because no one ever does. I told him, "While you're calling, I need to collect our property." And he said no way. "I want to talk to somebody other than you." I told him, "If you do not give me the property. I will call the police because I'm not going to fight you for this stuff." He said, "Go ahead." So I did. I decided to wait outside until the police arrived. It only took about five minutes. When the officer got out of the car, I explained the situation. I got the surprise of my life! The officer said, "So you're going to shut him down?" I said, "Yes." And the officer said with a sigh of relief, "Good." The officer said they receive more calls for this hotel, than any other business in the city. He went on to explain that the calls were not from the hotel owner calling about bus passengers causing problems. The calls were from bus passengers because the hotel owner was causing trouble! The cop said, "He refuses to give them their luggage. He refuses to give them their change. Crazy things like that." So the police department was pleased that I was closing the station.

The police officer asked me to wait outside while he went in to talk to the owner. As the cop walked in the front door, he pointed to the sign on the door and asked me if I had seen it. I told him I had. Right after the officer walked inside, another police car pulled up. I told that officer what was going on. And he went inside, too. Shortly, one of the officers came back outside and told me I could come and get our property. I started to load my van with the bus company property. He also had a couple of suitcases that belonged to customers. I took those, as well, and made sure that the customers got their bags.

The last item to take was the keyboard. We provided the agents with a keyboard that included a credit card swipe. When I asked for the keyboard, the agent said it was his keyboard. I told him it was not his keyboard that it was our keyboard because we provided it with the software and the credit card swipe. He said, "If you take a keyboard, what am I supposed to use?" I told him to use the original keyboard that came with his computer. He said he didn't know where it was. He asked me if I could come back tomorrow to allow him to have time to buy a new keyboard. Even the police officer started laughing. I said, "No. I'm not coming back here, tomorrow. When I leave here, we are done." I told him to try RadioShack. Maybe he could buy one there. I took the keyboard and walked out. The police walked out with me and thanked me, and I thanked them.

I received a call shortly after that, from the District Manager asking me what happened. I told him the story and he said he agreed. The funny thing was, during our conversation he mentioned several other businesses in the area as possible alternatives for the bus station. That told me that he had been to the station I closed, at least once. I was amazed. If he had been there, why wasn't he as outraged as I was? Why didn't he have my predecessor move the station or at the very least, close the bad one?

Without exception, that was the worst station I have ever seen anywhere in the country. I am glad I did what I did. No one deserved to be treated the way he treated people.

RJ

No Pictures

It was a busy Friday in September. On Fridays, we always had a lot of Job Corps students catching the bus to go home. Generally, we would have two busloads of students trying to go home. To give you an idea of how many people that is, one bus will hold 55 people. In addition to the Job Corps students, we also had a lot of weekend travelers.

Both ticket lines were full. The lines ran the length of the station. But there was no problem, we had the buses and the tickets were printing smoothly. Then all of a sudden, the line closest to the front door shifted to one side. Everyone looked around to see what was going on. A guy ran in and yelled, "Call the police!" I heard the man yell, and when out into the lobby to see what was going on. I asked the guy what was wrong. He said, "Call the police, this guy is crazy." Right then, another man ran up to him with a pipe in his hand. The guy DID look a little crazy to me. They were both standing in the doorway. The second guy yelled at the first guy, "You can't take my picture!" He told the guy if he didn't give him the camera, he would kick his ass.

I'm usually pretty good with calming customers down. I tried talking to the second guy and asked him to calm down just a little. He totally ignored me. He was locked on the guy with the camera. The guy with the camera said, "I didn't take a picture of you. I only took a picture of your license plate because you cut me off. I'm going to give it to the police and report you." The other guy tried to grab him. I stopped him. Then he reached around me and grabbed the guy again. At that point, I realized this guy was out-of-control. I told the ticket agent to call the police. I continued to try to calm the situation until the police arrived.

Two police cars arrived and the police jumped out quickly because they could see there was a fight. I explained to the police what the problem was and they tried to separate the guys to get their stories. The second guy, with the pipe, ignored the police when they said put the pipe down. The guy continued to yell, "You can't take my picture! Give me the camera!" He tried to pull away from the police and that's when they grabbed him. It took two cops to get handcuffs on him. They put him in the backseat of the car. He was under arrest. The cops told the other guy. He should not be taking pictures of strangers. Obviously, it was a bad idea.

The police determined that the second guy was high on some type of drug. He was in the back of the car still trying to get out when they drove away. It was one of the rare times when I actually felt my customers and I were in danger. The guy was totally out-of-control. I think he would have killed the guy if he had the chance. Dealing with the public is never dull.

RJ

Wake Up, It's a New Year

It was the second week of January. The joys of the holidays had finally worn off. Everything was back to normal, almost. The big bus company had 13 buses that it leased from the state for a dollar a year. If we took care of them, we could use them.

For the last two days, several schedules had been canceled because the drivers refused to drive. This particular day, all of the schedules for the state were canceled. The drivers were refusing to drive the buses because the license plates had expired. That's right; the license plates on all the buses had expired! The registrations expired in December and no one in the Licensing Department of the big bus company realized it. How could they not have realized it? That's their job. They are the Licensing Department.

Apparently, over the course of last year, several people in that department were laid off. Staff of 10 was now down to two. The drivers were not going to run the risk of getting ticketed for driving a bus with expired plates. Plus, a lot of the drivers simply looked for reason to give the company a hard time. This time, the company gave them a reason.

I received a call from the Licensing Department asking me if I could go to the state capital and register the buses. This was top priority because service had been canceled. Of course, I said yes. I was only an hour away and it shouldn't be a problem. The Licensing Department had called the State Licensing Bureau, so they knew I was coming. I looked on their website to find the address. On their website in red letters, it stated that they did not accept Visa. My company credit card was a Visa card, so I thought I could not use it. I called our Licensing Department and told them what I saw on the website. The lady told me, she had discussed that with the State Licensing Bureau and they were going to make an exception for us. I said, "Ok, I'm on my way."

When I got there, the office was not set up very clearly because of renovations. But I found the right person and told her who I was and what I needed. She went and got another lady. This lady had spoken to our Licensing Department and had everything ready. All I needed to do was pay for them. It was $1500. I went to the cashier and presented my company credit card. She said we do not accept Visa. I told her that an exception had been made because we were behind the eight ball. She left the window to check with other people. She came back and said I'm sorry, but no one can accept Visa. I went back to the lady that had helped me and she said she did not discuss payment methods with our licensing office. GREAT.

I called our licensing office and told them what the problem was. I reiterated that I had questioned this and was told it was okay. I asked our Licensing Department who they spoke with that told them it was ok. She did not have the name of the person she spoke with. So I asked them what they wanted me to do. They were at a loss. I told them I could put it on my personal card, but I wanted to be sure I would not have a problem getting reimbursed. The Licensing Department told me I would not have a problem. But because of this glitch, I didn't trust them. I called my boss just to make sure that I would not have any issues when I turned in the expense report.

I made the payment. Everything was fine. I had the registrations in my hand. I called our licensing office and told them I could take the new registrations right to the garage so they could be put on the buses. She said, "No, do not do that." She told me to fax copies of them to her. She would in turn fax copies to the Driver Manager. The Driver Manager would take them to the garage. Then the drivers could use the buses with the copies as temporaries. She wanted me to take the originals to UPS or FedEx and overnight them to the Chicago garage. The Chicago garage would then put the new tabs on the buses when they arrived in Chicago over the course of the week. I tried to explain to her that all the buses were in my town at the garage. If I took the registrations to the garage, they could put the tabs on all of the buses today. There would be no need for temporaries. She said she had been told to send them to Chicago and that's what she was going to do. So I said okay and I did as she asked.

It just seemed so unnecessary when I was going to be in the same place as the buses in about an hour. But, I was not the Licensing Department. Maybe they knew something I didn't. It seemed like a lot of extra work and money for something that could've been taken care of in a couple of hours. But, that's what makes it a good story.

RJ

Good to the Last Drop

As manager of the terminal, I've always felt that it was a good idea for the company to provide coffee for the drivers and employees. So I had no problem providing coffee, sugar, cream or sugar substitute for the terminal employees and the drivers. They could drink as much coffee as they would like while they were at work. It was fine by me. So I could not understand why a one pound can of coffee disappeared in one or two days when it used to last two weeks.

I decided to investigate. I asked all of the employees if they had any idea what was happening to the coffee. I hoped that bringing attention to the issue would stop the problem. I was wrong. I could not solve the mystery. So I decided to lock the coffee up when I went home. That wasn't fair to the employees that worked in the evening. But that was just the way it had to be until I could figure out what was going on.

One day we were a lot busier than normal. When it was time for me to go home, I just went home. I did not think about locking up the coffee. After I got home, I did think about it but it was not that important. I was not going back just to lock up the coffee. As I said, the day had been pretty busy.

When I walked in the station the next morning, the mystery was solved. There were 2 cups of coffee grounds covered up with a napkin sitting on the counter. Apparently, Jackson the long-term employee and heavy coffee drinker had planned to take the coffee home with him and forgot. I knew the ticket agent was not taking the coffee because she did not drink coffee. In the six months she worked there, she never drank any coffee. So I knew it was Jackson who was planning to take the coffee.

I was pretty upset. I could not believe he was stealing coffee! He could drink as much coffee as he wanted so there was no reason to steal coffee. There's no reason to steal anytime but stealing coffee just seemed so ridiculous to me. The next day, I told the employees what I had found. Of course, everyone denied that they had done anything like that. Since I did not have any proof of who actually had placed the coffee grounds in the cups, I just told everyone that they should be ashamed. I then decided that before I would leave in the evening I would make one pot of coffee for the evening crew. Once that pot was gone they would be on their own for the evening.

I know this is not the most interesting story. But, it amazes what people will steal, if they think they can get away with it.

RJ

A Little Champaign

We all understand how the corporate world works. We know from time to time there will be things that we have to do that we disagree with. But that's life. We also know in the corporate world, there can be people with very large egos.

Byron Hopkins had been a bigwig at corporate headquarters for long time. When he came out to the field, he expected to be treated like a king. Not a like corporate executive but a king. It was really kind of funny.

The company was rolling out a new express service. It was a great idea and had been successful in several parts of the country already. Now it was being rolled out in my area. We were all excited about it. I had briefed my agents on the importance of outstanding service when the express schedules came through their town. My station in Champaign was going to be the first commission agency to have the new service. I wanted everything to be perfect. But for some unknown reason, information about the new service was not given to me by the corporate office. The commission agent, I had in Champaign, kept me abreast of all the progress. When there were meetings concerning the service, my agent let me know and I would attend. It was very strange, but I figured with the rush to roll out the service, it was just one of those things.

The service started and was running perfectly. It had been running for two weeks without any problems. We got word that Byron Hopkins and several other bigwigs from the corporate office would be riding the new schedule. When that schedule arrived in Champaign, they were going to get off the bus and spend about an hour in Champaign meeting with the agent and just checking things out. Then, they would catch the returning schedule back to their point of origin. Of course, Champaign being one of my locations, my boss, Jim Dukes, called me and told me what time to be in Champaign to meet their bus. No problem, Champaign was an outstanding station and I knew they would be impressed. The new service was running fine. So it should've been a nice visit without incident.

The morning of the visit, I was driving to Champaign as planned. The visit was scheduled to be in the afternoon so I had plenty time to get there. I had not heard from anyone regarding the visit. I checked with the station they were scheduled to depart from and they had left on time. Great, everything was running as it should.

I stopped at a rest stop about an hour from Champaign. While I was there, my agent in Champaign called me and said she was told their plans had changed. They were no longer going to spend an hour in Champaign. They were going to spend about five minutes there and continue on that schedule. Jacqui Smith, my agent in Champaign, also notified her boss that Byron Hopkins would not be there for the planned meeting. I thanked Jacqui for the call because I had not heard anything from my corporate office. I was just about to call Jim Dukes, my boss, to confirm what I had just been told. But to my surprise, my phone rang. It was Jim Dukes. He said, "Trish Wardman (his boss) had just told him the plan had changed. Byron and crew were only going to be in Champaign for five minutes. And because of the short visit, I no longer needed to meet them in Champaign." I had another station closing the same day. Jim Dukes said, "Now, you can go close that other station." He even made a joke that sometimes we just have to jump through hoops for the bigwigs for nothing. I said, "I'm only an hour away, I can still make it, if you want." He told me, "No, there's no need to waste any more time." I said, "Ok, I'm turning around, thanks."

I should have known better. Dealing with the corporate office is never that simple. Byron Hopkins and staff made it to Champaign and stayed for five minutes, as planned. Jacqui Smith, my agent in Champaign, called me after they left. She told me everything was great. It was a quick visit, but Byron

Hopkins seemed to be quite pleased with what he saw. I told her, "That's great! Thanks for the great job." I didn't think any more about the visit. I was glad it went well but I was not surprised.

A couple of hours later, Jim Dukes called me. He asked me why I didn't meet Byron Hopkins in Champaign. I thought he was joking. I said, "What? You told me I didn't need to go." He said, "No I didn't." I said, "What's going on? Are you joking?" I asked because he sounded serious. So I asked, "What happened?" I thought that maybe something bad happened that my agent didn't mention. Jim said, "The visit was fine. Byron liked what he saw." I said, "That's great. The agent told me that, too." So I said, "I don't understand. What's wrong?" That's when Jim Dukes dropped the bomb. He said, "Byron Hopkins was pissed off because you were not there to meet him." I said, "No way, you have got to be kidding. Didn't you tell him that Trish Wardman told you I didn't need to be there because they changed the plan?" He said, "I can't tell him that. Are you crazy? Trish would have my butt. You know how big Byron's ego is. Now that he's pissed, someone's got to take the heat."

I said, "I don't understand what the big deal is. Everything was fine. The station was great, clean, the service work perfectly. Am I missing something?" He said, "No, you're right everything was fine, but Byron expected you to be there. He doesn't know that we knew he changed the plan. We don't want to upset him further. So I have to ask you a favor. Byron and Trish are going to send you an e-mail and ask you why you were not in Champaign. Trish is acting like she had no idea about the change. She told him I didn't know about it either." So I said, "You both are throwing me under the bus, even though you told me not to go." He said, "We're not throwing you under the bus. We are trying to keep the peace." I said, "Why not just tell the truth? Everyone knew he changed the plan." He said, "You don't understand. There's a lot more going on down here. Please do us this favor. I know it puts you in a bad light. But we will make it right, later. You have no idea what it's like in Texas when Byron doesn't get what he wants. He takes it out on everyone." I said, "This is crazy." He said, "You just don't know."

As I said, I should've known better. But, I did as he asked because he seemed so worried. He swore they would look out for me in return for this favor. To this day, Jim Dukes and Trish Wardman pretend that they have no idea why I did not show up in Champaign. I can't believe I fell for their lies. Oh well, we all live and learn. Cheers!

RJ

Strange Decision

Wendy had worked for one commission agent or another for at least 10 years. She was very dependable, very knowledgeable and pleasant. She worked at the current station for three years. The agent she worked for had given up the station. The new agent placed a high value on Wendy's experience. For the first two weeks, the new agent allowed Wendy to continue to work mornings. The new agent was actually a couple. A husband and wife team, Stacey and Greg. After observing the operation for a couple of weeks, they realized the station was not being run efficiently.

Without a doubt, Wendy was the most valuable employee they had. They did not want to lose her. As the actual business owners, it was important for the agent to be there during normal business hours. The station was open seven days a week for approximately 15 hours a day. The new owners knew they did not need Wendy to be there in the morning. To try to hold onto Wendy, they decided to allow her to pick any hours she would like. The only exception was Wendy could not pick the morning shift, because that's when the agents were going to be there.

Stacey and Greg called Wendy into the office. They told her how much they appreciated her hard work and valued her as an employee. They told her she was the best employee they had. But, they were going to work the morning shift. Stacey told Wendy, she could work any hours she would like except the morning shift Monday thru Friday. They told her to take some time and think about it. She could break her schedule up. She could work part time on the weekend, any combination that she wanted. They would schedule the other employees around her choices.

Wendy was surprised. She had just assumed she would work the morning shift forever. She told them that if she could not work the morning shift, she might have to quit. Stacey and Greg were quite shocked at her response. They reiterated that she could work any combination of hours that she would like because they valued her as an employee. She was quite upset and asked if she could have the rest of the day off to think about it and they said sure.

Financially, Wendy and her family were having trouble. The economy had taken a turn for the worse and her husband had been laid off. Wendy did not want to work any shift, except the morning. Despite the fact that they needed the money, Wendy stood her ground. The next day she returned to work, and gave Stacey and Greg her ultimatum. If they would not allow her to work in the morning, she would quit.

They were stunned. They knew about Wendy's financial issues and could not believe she would throw her job away. Wendy felt that she had been working for the bus company for 10 years and had earned the right to work in the morning. Stacey and Greg told Wendy that she'd only been working for them for about a month. They understood and valued her experience with the bus company. And that was why they were giving her total flexibility for her schedule. They did not want to lose her. But she could not work the morning shift. Wendy paused, looked down at the ground and began to cry. She looked up and said, "Then I have to quit." She handed them her keys and her swipe card and walked out. They could not believe Wendy had just quit over something so minor.

I was walking in the building right as Wendy was leaving. I noticed that she had been crying and asked her what was wrong. I had known Wendy the 10 years she had worked with the bus company. She stopped and gestured for me to follow her. We walked outside and she told me what happened. She said she did not want to quit, but she had to. When I asked her why she had to quit, she said she wanted to be home when her kids got home. I asked her, "Aren't your kids grown?" She said, "Yes." I hoped my question would make her see the light. But it didn't. She said, "It doesn't matter. It's my choice." I told her I did not understand why she was taking such a hard line with the new agent. I told her she should give them a chance to see how things go. And she said, "No. I've worked too long for this."

Most employees would love to be given the freedom to set their own schedule. It just didn't make sense to me. Maybe there was something else going on, but she never came back.

RJ

Law and Order

From time to time, I would have to attend a small claims case on behalf of the bus company. I found this case funny because the customer filed the claim in a city that had nothing to do with his trip. I think he hoped that no one from the company would show up because of this discrepancy.

The court recorder called for John Smith versus the bus company. John Smith approached the bench and so did I. John seemed to be a little surprised that someone from the bus company was there. We both took our prospective positions and agreed to tell the truth.

John Smith had traveled from Chicago to St. Louis. He claimed that the bus company owed him $2000 for the bag that he left on the bus. Now, there are two types of baggage. One is a checked bag, which goes under the bus and you receive a claim check for it. The other is carry-on baggage. And that's baggage you carry on the bus yourself. It is usually stored in the rack overhead. The bus company is liable for the checked bag under the bus. It is your responsibility to keep up with anything you take on the bus with you. This customer was filing a claim for a bag that he had taken on the bus with him.

Mr. Smith told the judge that when he boarded the bus, he put his backpack in the overhead rack. He said that in his backpack he had a laptop, iPod, CDs and a few other miscellaneous items. He said that when the bus arrived in Springfield, the driver said they could leave their items on the bus because they would be reboarding the same bus. They were only there for a 15 minute break. So, he left his backpack in the rack overhead. After about 10 minutes, he went back to the gate and saw the bus sitting there. He watched as employees swept out the bus and took out the trash. Then he noticed another employee got on the bus, started it up, blew the horn and started to back the bus out. He was surprised because the driver said they were going to reboard the same bus. As the bus drove away, he never said a word to anyone. A few minutes later, a different bus pulled into the same spot as the old bus. Shortly after the new bus pulled in, his driver came to the door of the terminal and announced it was time for passengers going to St. Louis to reboard their bus. All of the customers began to line up and reboard the bus. Once the bus was loaded, the driver made an announcement stating that the bus was going to St. Louis. Anyone not going to St. Louis should get off the bus. No one got off the bus and the bus left and went on to St. Louis. When the bus arrived in St. Louis, Mr. Smith got off the bus and went home. He never said a word to anyone about his bag. Two weeks later, he filed a small claims case with the court in Benton Harbor.

The judge asked him, why he didn't say anything to anyone at the bus station when he saw the bus with his bag on it back out from the station? He said, he thought the bus was coming right back. The judge then asked him when they started to board a different bus, how come he did not tell the driver his bag was on the other bus? Mr. Smith said he didn't know. The judge asked Mr. Smith, "Why didn't you say anything when you arrived in St. Louis?" He said, "I just wanted to get home."

When it was my turn to speak on behalf of the bus company, I basically reiterated the judge's questions. I explained to the judge that luggage that is carried on the bus is the responsibility of the customer. I gave the judge documentation that explained checked luggage is the bus company's responsibility and liability. I also reminded the judge that Mr. Smith said he did not tell anyone in any of the bus stations about his bag. When he saw the bus with his bag moving, he should have said something to someone. If in fact, the driver told the customers they could leave their items on the bus, Mr. Smith never alerted us to the mistake so it could be corrected. If he would've simply said something to anyone at the station in Springfield, they could've retrieved his bag from the bus. The fact that he left and did not report the lost item to anyone at the bus station makes me very suspicious. The first we heard of this lost bag was when he filed this small claims case. I asked the judge to dismiss this case because the bag on the bus was actually Mr. Smith's responsibility.

The judge agreed with me. The judge went on to tell Mr. Smith that it was negligence on his part to stand there and watch the bus that he knew his bag was on, pull away from the station without saying a word. If in fact he had a bag on the bus, he never made any reasonable attempts to regain his property. Therefore, the case was dismissed.

I was glad the judge agreed with me. I cannot believe the guy testified that he saw the bus leave with his bag on it and that he never told anyone about the bag, at all! Then he would go through the trouble of going to Benton Harbor which was not part of his trip from Chicago to St. Louis to file a claim. I think is a good example of a person trying to get something for nothing.

RJ

The Letter

Corporate headquarters received a letter from a customer that had received poor service in a small Wisconsin bus station. I happened to be at the station when the event took place and I agree that the customer received very poor service. I must admit, I was surprised at the poor service the customer received, as well.   The independent contractor involved in this incident no longer works for the bus station. Here is the letter.

To Whom It May Concern:
More often than not, customers riding the bus equate their experiences to a cheap tawdry affair replete with the low-level services you can expect from economy travel. But this is a different kind of letter. While I have a host of complaints to express regarding my experiences on December 23, 2006, none compared to the overwhelming sense of satisfaction I feel from the kind and supremely professional service I got from Robert Jordan, your Agency Sales Manager from Detroit, Michigan.

Here's why I'm smiling...
A few days before Christmas 2006, I was preparing for move across the country, from the small town in Wisconsin to Nevada and I needed to ship a mattress, a box spring and a bed frame. Exhausting all other overpriced shipping options for these items. I turned

to the bus company expecting the worst, but hoping for the best. Indeed, I got both.

Knowing that most of the clerk's in my local bus station are as capable as an experimental group of low order primates, I chose against calling ahead to assure this bed could be shipped and decided to go down to the station and communicate with someone face-to-face. There I was greeted by ticket clerk named Jamie, whose stone cold expression was more intimidating than welcoming. But from her, I was able to get the maximum dimensions allowed for shipment on the bus, even though was clear she had no real idea what she was talking about.

That day I returned home and called the bus company package express on their 800 number to be sure I was getting the right information. Of course I was not. The dimensions Jamie gave me were several inches smaller than the dimensions your company actually allows.

Mind you, I made all of these extra cautions to assure this bed could be shipped. Even though, five months prior I shipped this very bed from Virginia to Wisconsin without a single problem. Because your lethargic employees in my hometown lack not only the education, but the fortitude to handle something like customer service, I took every step to avoid wrapping up my bed, trekking it all the way down to the terminal and having them say, "Sir, we can't ship this."

But guess what? They said exactly that, except not nearly as polite. To make matters worse, I even walked into the bus station. Upon arrival with a bed atop my SUV and asked for a dolly, large enough to fit, well, A BED! Not only did they give me one, they helped me, wheel it to the door and carry it in the rest of the way.

It was then that my dissatisfaction shot through the roof. First, after dragging the bed into the terminal, I sat there for nearly twenty minutes waiting for someone to help me. Madison is a small town, fast service, is hardly ever a problem. Finally, a groggy looking white man with white hair and off-white teeth clomped his way over to where I stood with a measuring tape.

His name was Vincent and apparently someone in your HR department thought it would be funny to hire him as a manager. Vincent measured the bed, even though, by the look of his boorish scowl, I could tell what the outcome was going to be: We can't ship this bed.

I attempted to explain to Vincent. The steps that I had taken to avoid such a catastrophe but he scoffed, continued to be rude, cut me off and walked away while I was in the middle of a sentence. THIS IS NOT ACCEPTABLE. It is unprofessional. It is tacky and is why customers think of dirt when they think of buses because your reputation is perpetuated, if not heightened by imbeciles like this.

But this is a different kind of letter...

After Vincent disrespected me, and I assure you I never raised my voice, he attempted to disappear into an office nearby. I followed him and it was there that I found Robert Jordan calmly sitting in a chair, filling out paperwork. I asked him for his help and he said to give him two minutes. And he'll be right with me. Two minutes later, he was there...

Robert first measured the cabin on the bus, then measured my bed, which is exactly what the Virginia clerks did for me when I initially sent it from there to Wisconsin. The conclusion: The bed can be shipped. Even after Robert instructed Vincent to help me further, Vincent was combative and unwilling to listen, so much so that I refused service from him and asked Robert to complete the order. He did and not only that, he made sure every detail of the shipment was done with excellence. He wrapped the shipping tags tightly, so they wouldn't fall off. He double stamped identifying labels. He even printed out the manifest for me to have a copy. He was a consummate professional.

Four days later, my packages arrived, far earlier than I ever expected. I'm convinced that if it weren't for Robert's attention to detail and interest in helping the customer. I would not have my bed at all. This type of first rate service should be rewarded while the pathetic service I received from Vincent, the manager, should be duly noted and taken into serious account. Robert saved me that day from a man whose abrasive attitude is akin to a Brillo pad, which I'm sure does not uphold quality standards his superiors espouse. I'm not petitioning for him to be fired. Everybody's got to eat. But it is my hope that he will be reassigned to another job where he doesn't have to work with customers so readily. He obviously can't handle it.

Robert, however, deserves your utmost praises. I don't know him personally, and I'll probably never see him again. But this one act of customer care and sympathy is the only thing keeping me from never using your bus company in the future. You will be well served to listen to Robert's opinions on how to improve your company. Thank God he was there.

Respectfully,
Norman Clark

It was very nice for this customer to take the time to write the bus company with positive encouragement. I really appreciated it.

RJ

It's My Dad

Terry was an excellent employee. He was a young man in his mid-20s. He was never late to work, and always did a great job. His people skills were excellent, as well. The customers loved him. I was glad to finally have a good employee that I could depend on. I had a hard time finding good employees. It was a relief when Terry turned out to be such a good employee.

When I received the customer's complaint, I was surprised that it pointed to Terry. The customer was a female about 65 years old. She said she had ridden the bus for years, back and forth to Texas. This time when she arrived at her destination, a small town in Texas, she discovered the problem. She handed her ticket to the agent and asked him what time did her bus leave to take her back home. She figured, she might as well get the information while she was still at the bus station. The agent looked at her ticket and said, "Paula, when did you join the military?" She said, "I'm not in the military. What are you talking about?" He said, "Well, you have a military discounted ticket." "Military discount? I paid full price, $250." The ticket agent showed her the ticket. It clearly stated, "military discount". The price showing on the ticket was $169. The customer was pissed off. She told the agent, she would take care of it when she got back home. She would not let them get away with this!

When she arrived back home, she did just that. The morning after she arrived home, she called my office. She told me she had paid full price for round-trip ticket. But the ticket agent sold her a military discounted ticket. She said that she believed the agent took the $81 and put it in his pocket. She told me the date and time that she bought the ticket. And she described the ticket agent. All of the information she provided, pointed to Terry. It was cut and dry. If her information was correct, Terry stole the money. I asked her if she would come down to the station and simply walk through the lobby and see if the agent that sold her the ticket was at the counter. I would meet her at the rear of the building. Terry was on duty at the time.

She came right down to the station. She walked right up to the window and put her finger in Terry's face and said, "This is him! He's the son of a bitch that stole my money." As soon as I heard her yell, I went to the front counter. Terry did not say a word. But I could tell by the look on his face that he knew what she was talking about. I apologized to the customer, and I assured her that I would take care of it. I thanked her and gave her a voucher for her inconvenience

When the lady left, I asked Terry to come into my office. I asked him if it was true. And he said yes. I asked him why. He began to break down and cry. I was really surprised. He said he was sorry. His girlfriend was pregnant. And his father had cancer. They didn't expect his father to live long. So he wanted to bring his father from out West to see the baby before he died. So he had been doing this to get money to buy his father a plane ticket. At the time, our reports did not show any discounted ticket sales. (That is no longer the case.) I asked him how long he had been doing it. He said he'd been doing it off and on for a month. I asked him why he did not come to me and ask if there was something we could do. He said he never thought about it. Of course, he had to be terminated. He understood and did not give me any problems. He signed his write up, turned in his stuff and left.

It's a shame that a good employee lost his job for $81. We'll never know how much he actually stole. Now, he's unemployed AND his girlfriend is pregnant AND he cannot afford to bring his father home to see the baby. Just dumb!

Cold Night

It was 4 AM. We had gone to the garage to start the four buses we were going to use for the Job Corps holiday charters. Carla, the Driver Manager, and I wanted to warm up the buses before the drivers arrived. It was 10° in mid-December. We had our, MagLight, flashlights that could double as a club if we needed one. You never know what may be hiding on a parked bus.

We had two buses up and running. The buses were totally dark when we boarded them. When we boarded the third bus, we thought we heard something moving at the back of the bus. Just as we turned to see what it was........a driver came running up the aisle, pulling his pants up and buckling his belt. He said, "Hey, hey, what are you doing?" Like, he was security or something. When he saw it was us, he said, "Oh shoot, I thought somebody was trying to steal the bus." We asked him what he was doing on the bus. He had an odd look on his face. He said he had fallen asleep because he was worn out. Right as he was saying that, we heard something else moving in the back of the bus. I said, "Hey! Who's back there," and pointed my flashlight in the direction of the noise. I didn't see anything but assumed they were hiding.

We told him we were going to start the next bus. We would be back in 3 minutes to start this one. He was to get his crap and get off the bus and not do this again. He looked relieved and without thinking said, "Thanks, we'll get out of here."

Sure enough, while we were on the other bus, he tried to sneak a woman off the bus! That is so insane!! What woman would agree to sleep with the guy in the back of a cold bus in December? Even if she was a prostitute, you would think she'd have a better place to do her job. People never cease to amaze me. You never know what someone might do. Or where ☺

RJ

Who Needs ID

Prior to 9/11, the bus company did not require names on tickets nor ID to purchase tickets. The only time a person needed to put present identification was if they were refunding a ticket or their credit card was not signed. As with other forms of transportation, things changed significantly after the attacks on 9/11.

After 9/11, every ticket purchased had to have the customer's name on it. The funny part about it was that we expected pushback from the public. But the pushback never came. Surprisingly, everyone was cooperative. A few customers asked why we needed their name but once we pointed out that it was better security, no one had a problem with it. Every bus station manager in the country had the same idea. Although the policy never stated that we should ask for government ID, everyone did. And, the customers presented it. We all felt that it was the perfect time to require it since we had to ask for the customer's name. How else would we know if the names we were given were correct? It just seemed to make sense.

After about a month, the bus company's corporate office held a national conference call for all terminal managers. On the call, the upper management sternly told us that no one authorized us to require identification for ticket purchases. And we were to stop that requirement immediately. We were to continue to ask for the customers first and last names but no identification was necessary, nor could we ask for it. We were all shocked. All of the managers in the field could not understand why the corporate office thought this was a good idea. And several of us expressed that on the call. They told us that a large percentage of our business in the south and west came from illegal aliens. By requiring identification, we were forcing them to find other forms of transportation and losing business. At the time, the whole country was security conscious and we could not believe that the company would put sales above customer safety. Of course, time has shown no harm was done but it was still surprising to us.

Along the same lines, several locations had taken it upon themselves to ask customers for ID when they purchased a ticket with a credit card. The credit card companies contacted the corporate office and informed them that their credit card holders were not required to present ID when making a purchase. The credit card companies said that the bus company was violating their agreement and must stop immediately. Once again, there was a national conference call and we were told to stop asking for identification with credit card purchases. We were reminded that our ticket agents should be matching the signature on the back of the card with the signature made by the person at the time of the purchase. Both policies are still in effect today. RJ

How Could They

This took place in early fall. It was a nice sunny day and about 2 PM. This station was one of the intermodals that have become a popular in a lot of cities. The train stops there. As well as the intercity buses and the city buses. The lobby was rectangular shaped. The ticket counters for the buses and trains were at opposite ends of the lobby. The trains arrived on the back side of the building and the buses stopped in front of the building. In the center of the lobby was a small store that sold magazines, newspapers and snacks. The remaining area was seating for the different services. The restrooms were next to the bus ticket counter area. And the police station was next to the train ticket counter area.

2 PM was the busy time at this station. There were four buses and one train there at the same time. So everyone that worked there was busy. The store had a lot of customers. The train and buses were handling luggage and customers galore. The lobby was full of people.

Eddie was 20 years old. He was on his way home from college. This was his first year in college. His mom suggested he ride the bus. She thought the short bus ride would be a good experience him. The total trip was only four hours. The bus had stopped at the intermodal for a lunch break. They were scheduled to be there 20 minutes.

Eddie and the other passengers got off the bus, amidst the crowd of people milling around the terminal. Eddie went to the men's room. There were few other men in the restroom. When he started to wash his hands there was only one person left in the restroom. Eddie didn't think anything of it. When he reached for the hand towels, the guy grabbed Eddie and slammed him into the wall. Eddie fell down and got up quickly. As he headed for the bathroom door, the guy grabbed him again and pulled him back. This time Eddie yelled, "Get off me!" and pushed the guy back. Eddie yelled again, "HELP", as the guy grabbed him again. They began to tussle around the restroom. The strange guy was stronger than Eddie. Eddie continued to yell help at every opportunity he could. But no one came to help.

As they continued to fight, the door opened and two guys stepped in. They saw the fighting and turned around and walked back out. They did not tell anyone about the fight they saw in the restroom. The strange guy was now starting to get the upper hand on Eddie. He slammed Eddie's head against the sink Eddie fell to the floor. He had a gash in his forehead and his nose and mouth were bleeding. And the stranger continued to punch and kick him.

During the fight, at least four more people came into the restroom and turned and left. Not one person tried to help or call the police. In the lobby, there was one bench that was approximately 5 feet from the door of the men's room. There were seven people sitting on the bench. They all could hear Eddie, calling out for help. And NONE of them went for help! Don't get me wrong, I'm not suggesting they should've run in the restroom and stopped the fight. But at the very least, they could've told someone there was a fight in the restroom. Or, told someone a guy was calling for help in the restroom. But they did not do anything! I could not believe it! The lady that ran the store said that she noticed a lady crying on one of the benches, near the restroom. It turned out that the lady was listening to the guy beat Eddie to death. But she did not get up and tell anyone. As Eddie fought for his life, 10 to 15 people were aware of the beating and did nothing to help him. Absolutely nothing!!!

Finally, a 12-year-old boy walked into the restroom. He saw Eddie lying on the floor in a pool of blood. Immediately, the 12-year-old boy went to the bus ticket counter and told the ticket agent there was a guy laying on the floor in the restroom bleeding. The ticket agent called 911 for assistance. Then the ticket agent went to the restroom to see what was going on. And the ticket agent found Eddie lying on the floor.

The strange guy that had attacked him was nowhere around. 15 seconds later, the police were there. That's right, 15 seconds. Remember, the police station was right at the other end of the building. The ambulance came and took Eddie away. Eddie had been killed in the restroom! It took a 12-year-old boy to report what was going on in the restroom. All of the adults that heard or saw what was going on and did nothing should be ashamed of themselves.

The police could not believe that all of these people had heard and seen the fight and didn't report it. The police were very angry because they knew if any of the adults had said something Eddie might still be alive. The police interviewed everyone in the lobby. And that's how we know that all of these people heard or saw the murder of Eddie. They told the police that they had seen or heard the assault. While the police were interviewing passengers in the lobby, another 911 call came from the city bus garage across the tracks. Someone had broken in and was trying to steal a city bus. The thief was the guy that had attacked Eddie in the restroom. He still had Eddie's blood on his hands and clothing.

The police said the stranger had mental issues and attacked Eddie at random. It took five policemen to restrain and arrest him. Apparently, the stranger was schizophrenic. That is still little consolation for Eddie's family. And no excuse for the people that refused to help Eddie. We could not believe that people would sit there and listen to this young man call for help and not help. What was wrong with these people? How could they not help?

Of course, the bus and a train staff were worried about the negative publicity they would receive from the press regarding the murder. But the press took a different angle. The press focused on the insensitivity of all those passengers that did not help. They questioned society as a whole. They asked what was wrong with this town that no one would help the young man calling out for help. They were outraged!! A person was murdered in a public place with lots of people around, in the middle of the day, and no one helped the victim or called the police. How could they do that?

RJ

Good Business?

Several states around the country have a bus leasing program for intercity buses. Intercity buses are not city buses. They are the buses that take you across country to different cities and towns. This is how the bus lease program generally works. The state purchases "X" number of buses for a bus company based on how many miles the bus company runs in their state. The intercity bus companies then lease the buses from the state for one dollar per year, per bus. The buses cost approximately $500,000 each. The agreement includes a stipulation that the buses can only be used in that specific state for regularly scheduled service. The idea of the program is to ensure that citizens in the state have bus service.

In this particular state, the big bus company operated 15 buses under the lease program. It was a great deal for the big bus company. All they had to do was take care of the buses and they could keep running them forever. After a certain point in mileage, the buses would be replaced by the state. The big bus company, would in turn, purchase the used buses at a significant discount. The big bus company could not lose on the deal. But they could surely mess up the deal.

Over the years, several drivers and company employees had reported that the maintenance department was not taking care of the leased buses.

Sometimes, weeks would go by and every bus I would see in the state would not be a leased bus. Which would prompt the question, where were the lease buses? After a little investigation, they would be found waiting for repairs in the garage. This happened over and over again. Gradually, the state began to get word that the big bus company was not taking proper care of the buses.

The state inquired about the rumors and the big bus company ignored the state inquiries for years. It was so ridiculous!! A simple response from the bus company would've made the state happy. But the bus company chose not to respond. The state basically, gave the big bus company 15 buses and all they had to do was maintain them properly but they didn't care. They performed the minimum maintenance to keep them on the road. Despite the warnings from the field (drivers, employees and managers), the corporate office pretended there was not a problem.

Finally, in the spring of 2012, the state sent the big bus company a letter stating that the way the company had been maintaining the buses was unacceptable. The bus inspections conducted by the state had confirmed the rumors of poor maintenance were true. The state wanted an action plan from the big bus company outlining how they were going to correct the problem. If the state did not receive an acceptable plan from the big bus company by a specific date, all of the state owned buses would be confiscated.

NOW, the corporate office was concerned. The Senior VP didn't want to be the one to tell the CEO that they had lost equipment worth millions of dollars because he was careless. The concern had nothing to do with maintaining the equipment. The Senior VP didn't want to be the one to explain the loss. The Senior VP had been told about the problem for years, from the field employees, and chose to ignore the problem.

At this point, the corporate office wanted me to help fix the problem. I requested to see the contract that the garage vendor had signed so I could see exactly what he had agreed to do. That seemed like a reasonable starting point. But I was not given access to the contract. I worked my way through all of the red tape and made it to the Head of Maintenance. I naively thought he would be more than willing to help me, considering the gravity of the situation. WRONG!!! He refused to let me see the contract, too. I could NOT understand why MY company wouldn't let me see the contract. I simply wanted to make sure our garage vendor was living up to his end of the contract. The Head of Maintenance did admit that he had not seen the contract, either. He never did explain why I could not see the contract. I told the District Manager about the problem I was having and he laughed. He said, "They will never let you see the contract." I asked,

"Why not?" He said, "They just won't do it." He was right.

A mechanic and I were assigned to be at the garage, until further notice. We were supposed to make sure that things were running smoothly. I had no REAL experience with the maintenance side of the company. No one could understand why I was given this assignment by the Senior VP. I think I got it because I kept pointing out the maintenance problems. I have good mechanical aptitude but that's not enough (I felt) for proper maintenance. At least, I had a great mechanic to work with. After a few weeks, a lot of the petty issues disappeared.

In two weeks, the state was going to conduct a major inspection of their buses. If any of the buses didn't pass, they were going to take all of the buses they owned and would kick the big bus company out of the bus lease program. The Senior VP, Head of Maintenance and everyone down to the mechanic and myself descended on the garage. Of course, all of the buses passed the inspection. The state and the big bus company's corporate office were happy with the inspection results. Passing the inspection would keep the state off of their back for a while. A week after the inspection, everyone was sent back to the jobs they held before the letter was received from the state. A week after that, the maintenance problems began to resurface.

You would think after such a close call, the big bus company would make REAL changes to the system to prevent the same thing from happening again. You would think!

RJ

Smile for the Camera

The bus company leases property all over the country for bus stations. The bus company also has agreements with smaller bus companies to share expenses for the property when they use the same stations. The opposite is true when smaller bus companies own the property and the big bus company stops there, too.

Then one day, a game changer hit the freeways in the United States. This new bus company felt that it did not need to use bus stations or pay to use bus station property. They began operating by dropping off and picking up passengers at curbside. They avoided the need for ticket agents by selling their tickets online. Customers simply received a confirmation number that they gave to the driver, when they boarded. Of course, this operation caused uproar in the bus world. Plus, they were stopping across from businesses and bus stations without paying for the additional wear and tear.

One day, we received word that the new bus company was going to begin running service from one of our stations in a college town. They made a deal with the landlord, which was the college; they could stop on the property without paying as long as they did not use the building. If their customers used the building, they would have to pay their fair share like the other tenants. The big bus company objected to this agreement because no one would stand outside if the building was open. And any customer that wanted to use the restroom while they were waiting would use it. All the while, the costs for the new bus company would be covered by the big bus company. The big bus company knew that would happen because no one was going to monitor the traffic generated by the new bus company.

So, I was given the task to sit in the parking lot with a video camera and videotape any new bus company passengers going inside the building to use the restroom. I did not like nor see the need for the video camera. I asked why could not just report what I saw. Then the landlord could check and the new bus company would have to pay their fair share. The big bus company's corporate office wanted video footage in case anyone challenged what I said. I told them if there was a challenge, the challenger could simply come out and watch as I did. I thought it would be pretty creepy videotaping people going to the restroom. I also felt, if I was spotted videotaping people without their permission, they would kick my butt! But the big bus company did not agree with me nor did they care what I thought. They told me to sit in the parking lot, manned with my video camera.

As expected, the new bus company's customers used the building, just like all the other passengers. I really felt uncomfortable filming people walking from the new buses into the building. So, I only did it one day.

The crazy part was that even though the big bus company insisted I videotape passengers. They never wanted me to send them the footage. They took my word for it, which is what I suggested in the first place. The landlord confirmed what I reported by checking with the other tenants. As a result, the new bus company had to pay their fair share. I'm glad I didn't get my butt kicked for following the instructions of my bosses for nothing.

RJ

No He Didn't

It was a sunny day that wasn't busy. The bus was loading and there were only about 10 people getting on. Jake was the baggage guy. He had been working at the bus station for about 10 years. He had a reputation for being lazy.

The customers were putting their own suitcases under the bus because Jake was nowhere to be seen. As the last passenger put his suitcase under the bus, Jake was walking toward the bus. It was the only bus on the lot. When Jake got to the bus, he pushed that last suitcase through the baggage bin to the other side of the bus. The customers on the bus watched him walk around to the other side an open the baggage bin. They watched him take the suitcase off the bus. He carried it across the lot and placed it behind the trash dumpster. The passengers could not believe what they had just seen!! After they watched him come back and lock the baggage bins, they were sure he stole the suitcase.

One guy got off the bus and went in the terminal and asked for the manager. Security went and got the manager. The customer told the manager what they had seen. Jake was still standing at the side of the bus. The manager did not believe the customer. The customer then told him to go check behind the dumpster, if he didn't believe him. They all walked over to the dumpster. And lo and behold, there was the suitcase! The manager apologized to the customer and put the suitcase back under the bus. The manager asked a few other customers, on the bus, if they saw Jake put the suitcase behind the dumpster. The passengers all said, yes.

The manager had Jake come to his office. Jake got one day off without pay!!! I COULD NOT BELIEVE IT! He should've been fired for theft, at the very least. Not only did he get to keep his job, he was not written up for it either. WOW!!!

RJ

Acknowledgments

I'd like to acknowledge all of the hardworking dedicated bus employees and agents. Remember to smile. It will always make your day brighter. Do the right thing when no one is watching and you'll be fine.

I also want to thank my friends in the dance community for all of the positive encouragement. The only one that can limit you is you. There are too many things to see and do to stop now.

Thanks to my family. You are the foundation that keeps me strong. Without my strong foundation, I would have crumbled a long time ago.

Thanks to the mean, evil, lying and just plain hateful people in the world. Without your pitiful souls, the rest of us wouldn't realize how good life is (even on a bad day). Stop it and treat people better.

A special thanks to my little buddy Landry. You remind us all to take joy in the simple things in life.

Sigue Bailando!

www.ingramcontent.com/pod-product-compliance
Lightning Source LLC
Chambersburg PA
CBHW031514040426
42445CB00009B/223